AMERICA'S
DIVERSITY MELTDOWN

AMERICA'S
DIVERSITY MELTDOWN

Challenging Diversity Education and Its
Epic Failure to Improve Race Relations

John Fuller, Ed.D.

ARCHWAY
PUBLISHING

Archway Publishing books may be ordered through booksellers or by contacting:

Archway Publishing
1663 Liberty Drive
Bloomington, IN 47403
www.archwaypublishing.com
1 (888) 242-5904

Because of the dynamic nature of the Internet, any web addresses or links contained in this book may have changed since publication and may no longer be valid. The views expressed in this work are solely those of the author and do not necessarily reflect the views of the publisher, and the publisher hereby disclaims any responsibility for them.

Any people depicted in stock imagery provided by Thinkstock are models, and such images are being used for illustrative purposes only. Certain stock imagery © Thinkstock.

ISBN: 978-1-4808-3331-9 (sc)
ISBN: 978-1-4808-3332-6 (hc)
ISBN: 978-1-4808-3333-3 (e)

Library of Congress Control Number: 2016913716

Print information available on the last page.

Archway Publishing rev. date: 9/26/2016

Dedicated to my wife, Christine; without her entry into my life thirty-five years ago, this book would not have been possible.

CONTENTS

Small Keys Open Large Doors

Very small keys can open very large doors. The key's design must be perfect. One such key, which could have opened the door to race relations, was damaged beyond repair through the epic failure of diversity education. A new key is required. Americans have been indoctrinated by a completely controlled diversity education agenda for at least the last three decades. The result is America's Diversity Meltdown. "Us versus them" and "we need more of me and less of you" are unspoken themes du jour.

Minority activist groups refuse to respect opposing views or beliefs or to include white males in positive dialogue, choosing to confront and blame rather than work together for progress. The visual is becoming quite clear. Our country has failed to repel radical diversity education and, instead, merely accepts, without question in most cases, whatever diversity education is presented. We have failed to meet the increasing challenges of racial relations head-on by at least including discussion of race relations in diversity education. Without significant white male input or involvement with diversity education from its inception, the goal of positive race relations was doomed from the start. Instead, America is transforming and being retrofitted by social agendas, special interest groups, political leadership, and the courts—without the consent of the governed. America is becoming unrecognizable as the country I supported throughout my military career and lifetime. There are those who say that people who say something to the effect of wanting their country back are racists. That belief could not be further from the truth.

I want a country devoid of racial, ethnic, or religious animosity so that Dr. Martin Luther King's dream may someday, finally, be achieved. Historical issues of the past still echo and will do so or eternity. These echoes, though, are becoming pounding drumbeats each day with those who wish to resurrect history and believe the same context exists today. Agendas are packed with false narratives and rhetoric believed by many but based upon filtered or no facts. We American citizens need not concentrate our fears solely on a nuclear arms agreement with Iran, combating terrorists, ISIS, illegal immigration, or other events outside of our country. These issues and threats are without a doubt dangerous. Yet the real battle in our country rages with the meltdown of our American diversity experiment. We are currently and tragically undergoing what was promised by President Obama: the fundamental transformation of our country. Replacing our nation's experiment with this new model of diversity, emphasizing unquestioned support of special interests, is creating a nation unrecognizable by our Founding Fathers. Not only is the nation changing from their vision, many have forgotten the Founding Fathers themselves. Instead of continuing the formerly successful American melting pot with expectations of assimilating to the American culture, Americans are experiencing a diversity meltdown, due to non-assimilation of many immigrants who bring incompatible and possible volatile ingredients.

Participants attending diversity classes today experience self-described professionals who proclaim proudly that we are no longer a melting pot. That melting pot, they say, is old news. We are now, according to these educators, some sort of a "fruit bowl." I am not sure about you, but I would not like to be thought of as a part of a fruit bowl! In my discussions with participants in diversity sessions, I speak to inclusion with the mantra that it is all about us. The American experiment, if it turns completely into a fruit bowl, will be as the confounding languages were to the Tower of Babel: a complete disaster of unrecoverable proportions. Our nation increasingly exhibits this fruit bowl mentality in many locations; the ultimate result is what will be America's diversity meltdown.

America's ongoing transformation includes those who wish to prioritize their heritage identities, communities of color, assignment of "white privilege," and special-emphasis recruitment programs in employment for groups that no longer need them. Individuals choose to set themselves apart as unrepresented, victims, or incapable of enjoying the freedoms that our Constitution has bestowed upon them. People should be proud of their heritage, but put America first, and enjoy who they are now—as Americans.

When people encounter the word "diversity," they nervously maneuver around it or avoid the word entirely. It is as if it has no meaning, multiple meanings, or a mystical meaning—all of which can create, at times, confusion, agreement, conflict, or resistance. Some may choose not to mention the word at all for fear of being considered politically incorrect, misrepresented, racist, or somehow phobic in their views. Prior to the start of my diversity presentations, sometimes I hear participants speak with others and witness variable reactions, including anxious haughty laughs, scoffs, or smirks, as if diversity were a subject one should dismiss or joke about. Many of those before my class express to me that they have had all of this diversity stuff before. Most likely, some have developed these beliefs through their prior participation in mentally painful diversity classes. They merely want to get credit for what, often, is a mandatory class—and get it over with.

That is, until they participate in my presentation. I emphasize inclusion, I include white males in the discussion, and I offer a discourse they have never seen before. When a class sees me, a white male, retired military, and listens intently to my straight talk about this subject, they experience, many for the first time, how a true diversity class should be conducted. I enjoy watching them and noticing visual cues that indicate excitement about a topic they had previously avoided as much as possible. Many participants ask me afterward when I will return for another session and say this is the first time they have seen diversity presented in this manner.

I want to capture participants' imaginations and allow adult learners to consider key areas of diversity in a different way from what, quite possibly, they experienced with emotional pain before. Many older-generation participants have, unwittingly, experienced a countercultural revolution; that counterculture was and still is against white males. Curriculum designers designed diversity education not only to counter the existing culture but to transform it completely. They did so with concerted efforts and education that included invective references to retribution, blame, and disdain of white males.

Classroom participants sometimes experience educators who project a sanctimonious aura and who strongly believe that their twisted personal version of diversity is either the "right thing to do" or that they know what is meant by "getting it." No other word can create fear or joy, respect, resistance, or rejection—all within the same classroom—when this type of instruction occurs.

Polar-opposite reactions to my book are understandable. People will react depending upon their own situational experiences, historical reference, and prior learning experiences on the subject. When an instructor or writer uses straight talk, it normally and hopefully will resonate with some. Others may further contemplate this newly experienced and genuine diversity education. It is hard to penetrate the viewpoints of those who have had so many false narratives presented to them in the past. I have found, however, it is possible to encourage reconsideration of prior resistance to diversity when participants experience diversity education that is created to include everyone.

Given the history of diversity education, discussed later in greater detail, some participants may have endured extremely old-school and agonizing "diversity sensitivity" sessions where they were given exercises to explore their prejudices, biases, and feelings and basically made to feel terrible throughout the entire experience. Conversely, others felt good that certain others in the room experienced that pain! I know because I sat through them in the seventies, eighties, and nineties and, incredibly, this type of education continues into this century. Fortunately for those in my workshops, I remember that pain, and I told myself that if ever I was in a position to stop it, I would—and I have!

I experienced these excruciating diversity presentations of the past. When I experienced these classes previously while in the military, I remember scanning the room and noticed many participants who looked like they had just been startled out of a nap or daydream. How much learning transfer success could there have been? How effective in generating awareness or inclusion were these sessions? Instead of keeping with the basic meaning and principle of diversity, which is the understanding of the uniqueness of each individual, the word's meaning has transformed into an overemphasis on racial demographics (affirmative action), hiring (equal employment opportunity or EEO), and the myriad of special-emphasis programs which, in effect, divide and target differences while sustaining the "us versus them" theme of the last fifty years.

There is one exception. White males, especially, are expected to attend mandatory education in diversity classes, even if others including women and minorities find a way to not take these classes. This is especially true of "white managers," so they are able to properly leverage diversity—which is a code for managing minorities. We continue to hear, through classes, and see, in glossy company and federal program brochures and websites, that diversity is more than race, sex, and ethnicity, but that message is lost in the training and special targeting of minorities and women with the hope, dispelled later, that these efforts will increase employment percentages of these groups.

White males, in the aftermath of nearly fifty years of equal employment opportunity (EEO) and thirty to forty years of diversity training programs, still see themselves iced out from diversity and inclusion programs and discussions. Although I insist on inclusion rather than exclusion in presentations, the overwhelming number of other diversity educators (some inadvertently) convey to white males a message that is something like, "Hey, even though you don't feel that you discriminate, you actually actively support diversity, and treat each other with respect, you *still* must have discriminatory biases and actionable prejudice about minorities and women." The reason, they say, is that now you are just unconscious of it or demonstrate "microaggressions."

Microaggression is a subjective and interpretative nightmare term that some use to refer to unintended discrimination. Psychiatrist and Harvard University professor Chester M. Pierce coined the word microaggression in 1970 to describe insults and dismissals he said he had regularly witnessed non-black Americans inflict on African Americans. For some reason this term is now *en vogue* and has been resurrected for use in diversity education. The term has taken on new life, with "The Microaggression Project," which states on its website that it is "in solidarity with #Baltimore, #Ferguson, and #BlackLivesMatter. As we always say here, the micro only matters because of the macro systems of injustice."

If one is to accept the Project's definition, then the Project should accept an addition to the definition as quoted below. My proposed addition is that the definition of microaggression must also apply to the microaggressive actions toward white males by some women and minorities as well as those consistently reinforced throughout diversity education. You could easily replace "people of color" with white males when used in context with diversity education, in the past and today, with its loaded, veiled terminology still meant to inflict blame.

> *"Racial microaggressions are brief and commonplace daily verbal, behavioral, or environmental indignities, whether intentional or unintentional, that communicates hostile, derogatory, or negative racial slights and insults toward people of color."*
>
> *The Microaggressions Project*

The theory is that forty-five years and a generation of diversity education, since The Microaggressions Project was created, has not decreased the inclination of white males to be microaggressive! We as white males must be, to everyone else, a perpetually biased race; without any chance of ever removing that bias.

When women and minorities insist that "underground" discrimination exists due to microaggressions, it is without merit. Feelings do not equate to discrimination but to possible lack of knowledge or civility. It is the sincerely held belief, however, that discrimination, even unseen or unproven, must exist when it comes to white males. So the theory goes: white males will still discriminate, albeit covertly, and they are now just sneaky about it. White males it seems, even from the distant past, did so and forever will continue to discriminate against all others, no matter how they act, behave toward women or minorities, or actively support diversity.

Under that underground discrimination theory, those theorists would believe that I too discriminate whenever possible after presenting diversity education. What utter nonsense! How can someone, without being deceived, believe this literally happens—without any proof to support that belief? Do those who believe also believe in other conspiracy theories? It is, after all, closer to conspiracy than any sort of reality. These same individuals who do believe it certainly cannot claim to support Dr. Martin Luther King's message. Companies and federal agencies buy into much of this astonishing drivel without adequately vetting training materials. They hope they are doing "the right thing," and others are doing the same, using the same contractor, so at least they can check the box for training in this area. Corporations instinctively know that training will help mitigate future EEO complaints.

My perspectives, views, and recommendations presented throughout this book are through the lens of a dedicated diversity practitioner who has presented nearly a thousand educational presentations in diversity, cultural competency, LGBT awareness, and inclusion nationwide. My cultural experiences have been honed by twenty-two years of active-duty military experience in the US Army and Marines as a senior advisor and instructor for the Department of Defense Equal Opportunity Management Institute (DEOMI), a corporate EEO and ethics manager for Vance International which is a subsidiary of a Fortune 500 company; director of workforce diversity and equal employment opportunity for Johns Hopkins Hospital; and chief diversity educator for the Department of Veterans Affairs.

I will provide key considerations for diversity education which will, I hope, enlighten some or at least allow some re-examination and rational thinking in others. Straight talk usually sparks an internal response from people to think about a subject a little deeper (or differently) than before. It is my goal to further diversity as it should be, which is feeling absolutely comfortable with diversity and understanding that everyone is diverse. We are all unique, and we are all part of diversity.

I acknowledge that this book does not apply to all white males, minorities, and women in this country. We are way too diverse for that, with the myriad of learned thoughts, experiences, and attitudes within each person and in any race or culture. There will be those from all races and ethnicities who feel that they do not think or feel what I have written is correct or who vehemently disagree, but some facts are facts, and I will let the readers come to their own conclusions. As a white male and recognized champion of diversity in this profession for nearly three decades, I take on this mantle, to challenge inherently flawed diversity education, with resolve. There is much to be discussed before we all experience the meltdown of diversity in America.

"There comes a time when one must take a position that is neither safe, nor politic, nor popular, but he must take it because conscience tells him it is right."

Dr. Martin Luther King Jr.

CHAPTER 1

Genesis

America's diversity meltdown began with restricted pushback to original diversity curriculum in addition to acquiescence from nearly everyone. Some say this was largely due to white guilt. Some acquiescence may have been but I feel, more importantly, it was due to white male exclusion. I chose to use the word meltdown in the title of this book for, without a doubt, it is applicable. A nuclear meltdown is an informal term for a severe nuclear reactor accident that results in core damage from overheating. America's core meltdown is imminent. Through false narrative rhetoric and injurious diversity education forced upon others over the last three decades, America has been unable to protect its culture or increase positive race relations. Either through inability or unwillingness of Americans to protect our heritage, many have let extreme, outside special-interest groups redefine their American heritage for them. These groups do not represent the real values of America, yet have been able to take control without genuine debate or discussion or through nearly irrevocable court decisions. Decisions that attacked America's core support structures, including its national language, security, respect for borders, and culture;

areas that were already damaged. The meltdown also reflects the failure of far too many illegal immigrants who do not seek citizenship or, those who are legal immigrants, assimilate into American culture.

Significant changes including views, languishing resentment, and Americans' support for social causes that, even ten years ago, did not have broad support are all affecting our culture and wreaking havoc on our country. The term diversity still creates the same reactions as before, with the unusual range of agreement, rejection, confusion, anger, laughter, dismissive resistance, and many other emotions emanating from a mere whisper of the word.

From its inception, diversity projects the proverbial "white-male elephant in the room," and in the company of others, diversity can, to this day, trigger both positive and negative emotions. Unfortunately, in the twenty-first century, we have finally succeeded in corrupting the great American experiment with diversity. Or, more to the point, what others feel that diversity is or must be—to them.

Diversity, however, is infinitely more than race, sex, or ethnicity. It encompasses a broad spectrum of differences we all collectively possess and exhibit. In essence, it is a state of being and can be complex. Diversity includes the full spectrum of human differences, including but not limited to race, gender, sexual orientation, color, ethnicity, religion, age, physical and cognitive ability, socio-economic status, family status, lifestyle, organizational affiliation, and intellectual perspective.

More people than not, unfortunately, relegate the term "diversity" to merely describe race, sex, and ethnicity. This "inner circle" of visual perceptions is more easily formed in our minds. When we explore the dynamics of diversity within our organizational or community cultures, however, we see dynamics that go beyond just a few characteristics. When we look at additional dimensions of diversity, we see things that affect us each and every day, and much of it is right in front of us. But we may not acknowledge these characteristics as diversity dynamics.

What we observe, measure, or perceive is a lot easier to comprehend than a complex system of interrelated similarities and differences. All of these interrelated and interdependent attributes of each individual have to somehow work together and, we hope, form a synergy capable of performing a business task or project.

Envision an automobile with all of its interrelated and interdependent parts. Most of us just expect everything to work when we leave the house, open the door, start the car, and drive away. Little, if any, forethought is given to the engine (unless the warning light comes on) or the tires (unless one is flat) or the brakes (until we need to engage them). We all just unconsciously hope the car eventually moves when we start the engine, put it in gear, and push the gas pedal. If one does not pay attention and leaves the lights on overnight, the battery's power will drain. Imagine your dismay when you try to start the car the next morning. The quality of the engine, the newness of the vehicle, and so forth, makes no difference if the car will not start. Your turbo-charged car will just sit, silent, with no ability to move.

The same complex system exists within the diversity of each of us. We have some things that are readily observable, but most of our uniqueness is not. Some of these unseen qualities are our thoughts, perceptions, personalities, assumptions, visions, educational level, socio-economic status, veteran status, parental status, generation, gender identity, and sexual orientation, to name a few.

Many of the aforementioned attributes can have a significant positive impact in the workplace, or, if incompatible with others, pose a significant challenge and become problematic. Our brain does not give us a lot of help in this regard because many of our decisions about others are made quickly by the brain's amygdale in a split second or based on and confirmed by prior situational experiences. The decision made based upon these assumptions may or may not apply to the person we are observing or encountering. It is therefore up to all of us to take the time to seek first to understand, then to be understood.

Diversity's contributions to inclusion are highly dependent on the presence of facilitating or inhibiting conditions in the organization; absent facilitating conditions, the aforementioned desirable outcomes may not occur. An individual's uniqueness determines how that individual will think, behave and believe. Each of us has a unique lens through which we see the world around us and that influences the way we approach work, daily living, and opinions of others.

A diverse workforce fully reflective of America is truly not sustainable. It is not because of a perceived need for goals or unspoken quotas. The state of diversity in this country has become a function of existing demographic numbers of all facets of diversity in the country and the existing labor force. In an unusual twist, some universities and colleges now favor men by admitting them at higher rates than women, since women now make up nearly 60 percent of the student body. They are trying to preserve a male-female balance on campuses to achieve that elusive "diversity."

Stealthily acquiring as many definitions and associations as reactions over a period of thirty or so years, diversity also experienced byproducts of unexpected, undesired, and unwanted results. Silent codes and veiled words and phrases inserted into most diversity training sessions persistently perpetuate "us versus them" themes.

Many employers unwittingly and unconditionally accept these undesirable "magic words" as additions, without input from relevant and qualified subject matter experts, and without discussion or scholarly debate. Everyone else is using them so we must, goes the thinking of employers. Thus, over the years, they have accepted whatever the next veiled version is, thereby aiming to cover the bases of needing diversity training; this is still happening! I wonder if they would do the same for any other area of their business or agency, such as a new IT foundation, safety program, benefits, or other essential programs when considering profit and loss. I assure you they would if they felt it would affect the profit margin. It is unfortunate for many that they do not know that diversity does affect the profit margin.

> *"Diversity training in the corporate arena has a checkered history and a plethora of critics who are convinced that such efforts are a waste of time and money."*
>
> Mary Francis Winters, the Winter Group

Jacqueline Woodson, a noted children's book author and winner of the Coretta Scott King Award, states, "Diversity is about all of us, and about us having to figure out how to walk through this world together." This is a simple but genuine statement and an extremely powerful one. Others, including self-appointed civil rights activists, accept additions to their diversity terminology if, and only if, these additions support their agendas. Some activists are genuine in their intent but too many others are charlatans who paint self-portraits of their inflated importance.

If I were to ask one hundred people in my classroom audience the question, "what is diversity?" I would receive one hundred similar, same, or slightly different answers. Similarities and interpretations will vary, but all definitions have a similar foundation. A participant's level of exposure to overt and now covert "us versus them" diversity classes creates that foundation.

Diversity in the late 1980s became more of a nice euphemism inserted into corporate and educational institutions' strategic plans. They proclaimed that they actually wanted more people of color (except white) and women in their businesses or schools. The beginnings of "us versus them" themes were enhanced by institutional support for diversity's necessity and inevitability.

When there is controlled curriculum, there is also restricted interaction between people with opposing beliefs. Misunderstandings and mistaken assumptions often lead to conflict without open interactions. I see this in the EEO arena with multiple sexual-harassment complaints and other rising EEO complaints from males. Established through curriculum designers from the outset decades ago, diversity education severely affected the attitude of white males, which only increased their silence and resistance. An aggressive, closed belief system previously was abhorred by women and minorities, since they felt they were not included by the "dominant" culture. Unfortunately, women and minority activists' newly enhanced closed belief system has become the tactic they now advocate for their own purposes, excluding white males, for the most part, whenever possible.

All groups should be able to coexist peacefully, influenced by a variety of factors; the prevailing level of tolerance and respect for diversity, perceived threats, historical experience, new events, quality of leadership, and cultural custom. Groups instinctively can relate to each other with regard to diversity. Open civil discourse will deeply influence the flow of ideas and values between them. More often than not, white males vs. women and minorities in this country have not accomplished a balanced, positive relationship.

Six Year Odyssey

As the current chief diversity educator for the Department of Veterans Affairs since 2010, I embarked on what was to become a six-year diversity educational blitz for VA facilities across the country. Riding the trail to who knows where, from coast to coast. Anchorage, Alaska to Augusta, Maine, from Waco, Texas to Fargo, North Dakota, and countless flights and hotels in between. I was informed by my boss on the first day that I was to be the first "face of diversity" for the VA, the second-largest federal agency. I had been a "first" in the diversity world before—completely contrary to the established norm, the face of diversity for my federal agency would be male and white. I would make the supposition that not too many organizations could make that claim.

My mission is to present, through educational workshops, the subject of cultural diversity and inclusion as part of our strategic plan to provide this training for all VA employees. I brought to this mission a comprehensive background in diversity and EEO and an unparalleled work ethic created by a career in the Marines and Army. Nearly all VA facilities I visited had never received training from the Washington, DC, central office. Many facilities were in far-flung rural areas of the country. This clearly was a window of opportunity to provide connection to field employees who felt that the VA was not merely disconnected—it had never been connected at all. I would also be able to bring back each individual facility's pulse to central office from executive summaries derived from listening sessions with employees and management.

Facility pulses consistently reveal a myriad of emotions from all diverse employees including their likes and dislikes, frustration, anger, and many others. It is always rewarding to achieve their confidence. I am privileged to work with dedicated VA professionals in the field who are working not only with their own diversity but the diversity of all of the veterans they serve. Clearly, they had heard the voice for the higher calling in their careers and had the passion and valor to continue. Throughout over 650 presentations in forty-seven states, and with thousands of employees, I have held sessions for people from all walks of life, all races, ethnicities, sexual orientations, educational levels, parental statuses, all generations, religion, politics, and abilities. Who could ask for more as a diversity professional? The adrenaline that flows through me keeps the passion burning to create equality and respect for all.

I have observed something that is particularly noteworthy in all facilities in the past year, since the VA crisis started: The majority of VA employees maintain unwavering dedication to veterans, in spite of obstacles and barriers they cannot control. These are barriers other than discrimination, such as logistical and leadership failures, i.e., secret patient waiting lists, backlogs of claims, troublesome employees, and a percentage of simply horrible managers.

Through it all, most have persevered—some say because of their diversity, others say because of their integrity. Their survival in the VA is compelling, since their diligence while experiencing an untenable situation is remarkable. Survival in an uncivil work environment that sucks the air out of a room takes special courage from employees; this courage is derived from their being the best of the best. I salute my colleagues. Many times, these employees are required to muster tolerance beyond what a person with lesser values exhibits; this is not easy.

I witness diversity in action and at its best when conducting training in the field. I surveyed employees, using a specially developed instrument, for the purpose of requesting their input on their facility's pulse: gauging the attitudes of employee, management, and leadership. Approximately 10-15 percent of the VA employees, management, and leadership should get the heave-ho and be let go, according to VA employees—and many in Congress would agree. While that may seem like a small percentage, it amounts to about thirty to thirty-five thousand employees; since most of these individuals remain, they directly contribute to the organization's own diversity meltdown through their unjustifiable treatment of others.

On a positive note, employees expressed their gratitude that I came from Washington, DC, and they, for the first time, experienced a diversity class that was engaging and inclusive for all participants; no us-versus-them in my class! I also championed, during this period, LGBT awareness by either having separate classes in this subject or including this group in regular cultural competency classes.

No other person in my office volunteered to present LGBT awareness when it started to become an issue of inclusion throughout Veterans Administration hospitals. I understand some of the reluctance, since it is a topic that many outside of the LGBT community feel uncomfortable with presenting or to which they may have religious objections, and therefore feel unable to present. Regardless, after my experience presenting training and sharing this awareness, many have expressed their appreciation for including LGBT awareness, since it brought to their attention an emerging cultural area with which they were not familiar, and that was never discussed or they had never sought to understand. That is why I keep in the titles my courses "Key Considerations." I want people to possibly reconsider their beliefs about diversity; some of which have been previously presented to them in an "us versus them" theme.

I also receive comments from participants after classes, from minorities, women, and white males alike. Their comments expressed comfortable feelings about finally having a white male present diversity training. I felt this reaction strongly in areas such as Billings, Montana; Sheridan, Wyoming; Salt Lake City, Utah; and other places that have super-majorities of white demographics, as well as in New York City, Houston, Los Angeles, and many others with reversed demographics. People really do want a conversation with straight talk, not BS, and not with any hidden agenda. When we are finally able to do this throughout the diversity profession, we may have enough fortitude left to reverse the factors that have contributed to the impending diversity meltdown.

Affirmative Action's Impact

Affirmative action became one of the incompatible additions tossed around in the melting pot. Affirmative action itself was a noble goal at its inception, with programs to increase women's and minority representation in the workforce and eliminate documented employment and educational discrimination. John Kennedy, prior to the Civil Rights Act, wrote that the country needed to take affirmative action ensuring everyone had an equal opportunity for education and employment. Affirmative action then crept unnecessarily into the diversity profession and became part of training. One either had to support it or be considered to somehow be racist if, for example, one disagreed with it or thought it should be modified with the times.

Affirmative action today consistently strips away any resemblance of equality through its undesirable evolution from creating equality to a numbers-driven quota-like system for employment. I recognize that many will state that quotas are illegal, but they are being deceived. They are quite right in one regard: quotas, as in requirements to hire specific numbers of minorities and women, are now illegal (they were not in the past). Corporate and federal contractors, however, are expected to maintain affirmative action plans and list their "good-faith efforts" to achieve racial equality in their respective organizations, regardless of applicant quality or whether a targeted applicant is the best qualified. Numbers, however, are typically the focus of most conversations regarding affirmative action.

In essence, quotas are merely masked and referred to as either achievable goals or catalysts. Then there will be specialized programs that will address "barriers" when certain numbers do not match expectations in organizational employment. Workforce analysis teams of federal agencies, for instance, working in tandem with special-emphasis programs, work diligently to display the barriers to employment supposedly suffered (or historically suffered) by women and minorities. Special-emphasis recruitment and retention programs then target outreach recruitment and cater only to women and minorities. Their only purpose in addressing these barriers in facilities across the country is achieving the elusive end result of increased percentages of "expected representation" of women and minorities. Sometimes, those who run these programs can merely guess at what a barrier to women and minority employment might be; they primarily rely solely on "numbers." White males are excluded, even if their percentages (or numbers) are not what would be expected given their qualifications or are not representative of their percentage of the population. If that is not a quota-driven system by another name, supported by funding, and only for women and minorities, then someone at the Office of Federal Contract Compliance Programs (OFCCP) or the Equal Employment Opportunity Commission (EEOC) should let all of us in on the secret of what this program actually is.

Visualize diversity as a hard drive on a computer. Affirmative action plans, unfortunately, became intertwined with diversity and became a significant virus that was never removed, much like baggage fees on airlines today. Companies focus on compliance mandates from existing employment laws. Therefore, their affirmative action plans become important, time-intensive documents showing "good faith efforts" to increase demographic representation.

Reporting requirements, with possible audits by the OFCCP, also looms large in the minds of all federal contractors. That is because the OFCCP can sanction or shut a business down when it is not achieving goals (quotas) at the pace expected or cannot show good-faith efforts to achieve desired success. Federal contractors must submit copies of their affirmative action plans for any government bid; these are examined thoroughly. If "good faith efforts" are not being done, the sanction letter begins.

Demographic representations are routinely displayed in diversity discussions and presentations. Note that affirmative action plans include everyone with the exception of white males, since white makes have not been and are not considered a "protected category." White males, however, will soon be in the status of protected category, since their percentages are either at or below the "expected" range of participation that affirmative action plans demand in locations throughout the country. What will be done? Will a visionary leader create programs for white males that encourage their recruitment? We will see, but I sincerely doubt that it will occur in my lifetime.

"Us versus Them"

A workplace that values diversity is one in which all individuals in the workplace are treated in a fair and non-discriminatory manner. The initial step to achieve this goal is to establish a work environment where there is zero tolerance for any kind of harassment or discrimination. Unfortunately, compliance—not straight talk—is exactly what has occurred—and still does occur—in most diversity classes and programs, a situation that excludes and targets white males. White males' unspoken yet perpetual exclusion prevents encouragement of civil discourse or much needed critical conversations.

Restricted and unchangeable agendas were thrust into diversity curriculum, discussions, and training. Curriculum designers accomplished their goal of continued accusations of "white-male privilege," which basically eliminates any chance that most white males will accept the curriculum. Most white males idly participate in sessions where the curriculum has been established by minorities and women with unspoken agendas. Unfortunately, this "diversity world" of education remains today. I can see the look in the eyes of participants when I come out as the instructor; for many, it is the first time they have seen a white male facilitating a diversity session—and their first session without an "us versus them" theme.

Many educators will issue a disclaimer at some point in the presentation that diversity applies to everyone. The statement itself, however, is not sufficient in the training arena. Well-intentioned colleagues may think otherwise, but the existing curriculum remains totally infused with "us versus them" themes. The only difference in material with "new and improved" titles is a few words and *en vogue* phrases.

Why would anyone continue to present training sessions perpetuating this nonsense instead of attempting to eliminate racial, ethnic, and sexual discord with discussion on these issues? The answer to this question is very simple. Many younger diversity educators starting out today, for example, do not recognize that the original diversity training foundation was flawed from its inception, driven by a counterculture agenda. Nor are they aware that modifications along the way repackaged existing material with mere aesthetic enhancements. Training retains much of the social reform curricula from the 1980s. Those curriculum developers failed to realize—or, more likely, they intentionally developed a permanent and negative effect on white males with "us versus them" as a foundation.

Without an educational oversight governing body for the diversity profession, certification requirements for trainers, or an accepted curriculum, disjointed education was predictable and inevitable. If one takes a critical look, the original curriculum speaks volumes with its vigilante style; it is packed with stinging material directed at white males. If one takes the same critical look today, they would see the same—only now with a cloaking device masking the flaws.

Most diversity curriculum designers have been women and

minorities; this is still true. Many of them were originally pressed into the training arena without any guidance as to how diversity should be taught and with limited or no curriculum design experience. Only women and minorities were trainers, so the closely held belief goes, since white males certainly could not understand discrimination since, according to the presenters and special emphasis advocates, it is impossible for a white male to be discriminated against! Many were then able to weave in their biases, based on personal experiences of inequality and underrepresentation in education and employment, without check or debate. White males would not dare to question them except under their breath or away from the classroom, for fear of retribution.

The historical fact is that the original designers were also selected through what should be called a discriminatory litmus test. Most (regrettably) felt at the time, and now, that an instructor had to have experienced discrimination or harassment or, at the very least, be a minority or a woman; otherwise, the instructor would not have credibility with the audience. This judgment assumed that white males never experienced discrimination or harassment and therefore would not know about it. Of course, they had "white privilege," so it would be inconceivable for a white male to teach diversity or EEO. What absolute and unfounded baloney! My career, for example, has disproven that theory. White males were made the culprit in these sessions. That "white-male elephant" has never left the diversity training room, though, and it even takes me some time to remove it from the atmosphere. I understand those feelings and always endeavor to quickly change the tone of my classroom from what participants may have experienced in other classes.

Concerted efforts infused inequality, along with themes of "underserved," "underrepresented," or "white privilege" into presentations. Each of these terms, as used in the curriculum, purposely excluded white males and created what designers wanted, which were "white guilt" reactions. Present-day programs are simply redesigned programs of the past, with some newer "bells and whistles" designed to make the presentations more appealing and successful at evoking white guilt. White males, many presenters felt, had to get in touch with their feelings, since they were in denial and living in a fairy-tale land before attending the diversity class.

Additions to the training include *en vogue* words, phrases, and graphic charts; attendees can sit back and experience new-and-improved diversity training—but in the end, most likely, they get the same old tired and painful messages. The white-male elephant atmosphere remains in the room, primarily because the curriculum remains the same. Course content maligns white males, which many of its designers feel is unintentional (or justified), but those same designers expect the agreement of white males to what is being taught! There can be no dissension, so now only miserable silence from those who disagree. The end result is that most white males sit silently; they do not normally participate in these classes—unless they are in a class like mine. Diversity education's failure is extremely unfortunate since there is a compelling need for open discussions that include hard topics like race relations. Critical conversations are perpetually eliminated from training. Diversity professionals display a lack of confidence and stick with new words and phrases that they feel comfortable using. They just do not want to open a Pandora's Box and instead hope the box remains closed.

When diversity education crept into organizations, programming "training" was not seen as providing a return on investment. Only since about the turn of the century have businesses and organizations taken diversity seriously as a strategy. Organizations that used similar methods to address any crisis other than diversity were bound to find them insufficient and inappropriate. The organizational leaders were not prepared, which created inappropriate and ineffective responses through education. That was mainly due to an unexpected anomaly that had noticeable effects:

the new, unexpected, unrecognized, and unanticipated crisis on the block was this diversity thing. This was uncharted territory for all organizations, and strategy dictated not only a preliminary plan but back-up alternatives. Both were quickly needed to achieve non-traumatic transformation with diversity. The strategy must have as the end goal a willingness to be proactive, experiment, and achieve eventual buy-in from participants though discussion, civil discourse, and understanding. One experiment should have been using an ongoing team-building method to progress through stages, rather than directed, mandatory training that aimed to cure all ills in two hours or less. Risks needed to be taken with diversity education and failures adjusted with alternatives and next steps. Unfortunately, the "next steps" were in the same footprints, and failures were accepted and continually enabled.

The entire diversity training culture, due to its leaderless beginnings, evolved into a complex set of shared assumptions held generally (but not by all) women and minorities. Through inappropriate, calculated strategies of excluding white males from much-needed civil discourse, a magical destination or end point never was discussed. We, as white males, could not even discuss whether that destination *could* ever exist or why it *should* exist. We were to forever be suspended in time and could not move forward, with entrenched, combative diversity sessions and history lessons dedicated to increasing our guilt and recognizing our "privilege." Leaders of organizations, responsible for administering diversity training, should have realized that there was a possibility of hidden agendas, identified them, and found productive alternative approaches. Due diligence certainly was not part of any approach for diversity education. Would these same leaders not insist on due diligence for other areas of their organization? Or would they merely take a gamble and accept potentially disastrous training in the hope that, this time, it would "solve" the problem?

Using sports analogies, I refer to penalties given to players for unsportsmanlike behavior on the fields. While everyone recognizes that penalties occur in games, most penalties, like most mistakes in an organization, are not premeditated. Those that are intentional, however, are considered flagrant penalties. Think of a soccer match; the red card is normally reserved for the most flagrant fouls and results in ejection from the game for the player who committed the foul. In football, flagrant fouls (yellow flags) are usually intentional, such as piling on a defenseless tackled player after the referee has signaled the play is over. It could also be sacking (or tackling) of an NFL quarterback when the quarterback has already released the ball many seconds before. With diversity education, these red cards or yellow flags should be thrown all over an organization that uses current diversity education methods. Current educational methods, whether intentionally, unintentionally, or blatantly, increase the changes of the meltdown in and of themselves. The bottom line is that inclusion must include white males.

Diversity education, instead, was assigned to developers with carte blanche empowerment—and the developers came loaded with "hidden agendas." The developers were not honest in dealing with organizational leaders or with themselves. For this reason, existing diversity educational culture was conceived and merely rebuilt over decades. The culture, as I have experienced in the past, will not be easy to change, unless everyone is provided with straight talk and those who do the straight talk act with integrity. The recurring and perpetual nature of attitudes and feelings resulting from the aforementioned educational development of hidden agendas eroded American diversity. This erosion has now exposed its obvious flaws. Many flaws have their origins in the inappropriate and unfair diversity training that related only to portions of the audience by refusing to engage white males in respectful but challenging conversations.

"Getting It"

Don't you get it? That person does not "get it." Attendees on their way to diversity classes are already primed with preconceived ideas from prior mandatory classes. Attendees also assume that the class will be taught by a subject matter expert and at that the facts presented will be valid. They then listen to a false narrative of "us versus them" and eventually may say they "get it." In reality, what are they getting? Will years of diversity training be reprogrammed with a new "twist" on the material? It seems like some people believe that all you need to do is hit the refresh button or add new software for complete understanding, and two hours will do the trick!

The word "diversity" appears throughout public and social media, including in political and employment advertisements, professional magazines, scholarly literature, and so forth. An incorrect assumption is that almost everyone understands a precise definition of diversity. Another false assumption is that if someone does not, then after attending a diversity class, they will "get it." It would be great to meet the person who finally defines diversity's definition so I too can "get it." I might be able to take a deep breath and say mission complete; I doubt it!

Instead of being proactive, an excessive amount of diversity training is driven by a crisis, i.e., a lawsuit or investigation with a finding of discrimination. A court or EEOC finding of discrimination may require companies to provide diversity training to blanket employees with "get it" education. Courts or the EEOC must believe that no one "got it" before their mandate. Employers typically react quickly with mandated training just to meet compliance expectations, and most of the time, they do not use insight or review the training itself.

Numerous colleagues of mine and others repeat a standard expression: "Diversity is the right thing to do." Much to my chagrin, when I hear this phrase, I wonder if they understand what they are saying. Do they actually believe or understand the meaning of this phrase? What is right or wrong about diversity? What situation or to whom are they referring? Emotional responses to this particular phrase are often shaped by attendance at decades-old "us versus them" training.

The imperative challenge is to proactively promote diversity training and present it without purposely or inadvertently targeting others. Many educators are very passionate about diversity, but their training programs do not support that passion. Imagine daydreaming about riding a Harley but actually riding a 50cc scooter to work. Diversity curriculum exists today in a state of total disarray and is in desperate need of a major course correction. What is being delivered today appears to be more for contractors, who want to sell their product, rather than for the recipient or company that is exploring how this subject can benefit its bottom line or employee engagement atmosphere.

Selected training may either forgo a vetting process of material or contractors selected for required compliance training or may be extremely limited. The courts do not mind who gives the training, as long as it is provided. Would employers choose to forgo vetting for other vital aspects of critical areas of their business like safety, IT, or security? Employers select self-styled diversity contractors who typically do not have the requisite abilities or even knowledge of the employer's business but do have the lowest price or contract bid. Mandated training does not usually go over well with employees under any circumstance; this is particularly so when education promotes "us versus them" themes. "Us versus them" is the single most significant silent code restricting acceptance and diminishing inclusion.

Employees may feel that mandated training does not apply to them and they are just checking the box. Comments such as, "I already know this diversity stuff" or "Didn't we already have this course this year?" many times permeate the atmosphere before a session. Essentially, employees feel that it is a waste of their time. In that situation, is a person likely to feel that is effective or is that person going to just want to get it over with? The only benefits employees will "get" are boredom, loss of their time, and loss of productivity for the company. It may also increase employees' personal level of resistance to any future diversity training.

Encouraging employers to be proactive has been a daunting task for diversity educators. I realize that time away from the job is a critical consideration, but one must consider all factors. Regrettably, diversity training has long had a reputation of being something that is required rather than something that a company or its employees need or want.

Where Is the Elusive Final Destination?

"We have come a long way, but we have a long way to go." These words are often regrettably echoed by diversity training presenters or keynote speakers at diversity conferences. This long-held and worn-out phrase, and similar ones, is routinely spoken during diversity programs, seminars, and lectures. Predictably, at some point during a presentation, the speaker will state, "We need more diversity," or "We have come a long way, but we have a long way to go." These phrases have been a part of diversity training through-out my career and seem to be exclaimed on cue from a continuing loop of PowerPoint slides. As an educator and keynote speaker, I have never expressed any of these phrases during workshops or conferences. I prefer to achieve credibility with straight talk focusing on the way forward. Other speakers, however, seem to instinctively know they will have to utter these phrases to attain credibility with some attendees. Their unstated purpose though is to also create white guilt.

One of the most irritating phrase to me is the *long way to go* comment used in diversity training or lectures. The speaker never reveals to participants how long they still have to go or where they have to go. They actually have no real idea what they are saying. What or where is this magical destination, one may ask? Someday,

I would really like to program this destination they are referring to into my GPS. I do not know of a speaker, leader, or colleague who ever follows up this comment by revealing the mysterious destination. It makes one wonder if there is an actual end point to the "struggle." Should there be a destination, as advocated by visionaries like Dr. King? Are we expected to keep going on aimlessly without that proverbial light at the end of the tunnel? Never achieving the mystical destination is fantastic news for diversity contractors and speakers, who would prefer to keep it that way. If we all arrive at this final stop, they will be out of a job!

The diversity profession cannot hope to achieve even marginal success if my colleagues continually perpetuate the same divisive messages. We must remove any barriers to inclusiveness in our curriculum. As is evident in Ferguson, Baltimore, et al, we can still lose the quest for judging people by the content of their character by maintaining an "us versus them" posture.

Professionals in the diversity profession insist on adding demographic depictions of underrepresentation in charts. Why add this subject matter to presentations meant to represent uniqueness and achieve inclusion? Displaying demographic percentages is always going to be a silent code for "us versus them" or "we need more of me and less of you." Far too many self-styled "subject matter experts" from academia and business create even more confusion and resentment by inserting invented terms or enhancements to diversity. Some academics also write newspaper columns or academic papers that are divisive at best carrying a tone throughout that is invective. Many of these self-styled experts have never been associated with the diversity profession.

Barriers

Diversity applies to all—or does it? That depends on the presentation and what people believe. No matter what participants hear in a classroom, I see an overwhelming and embedded belief that

Diversity = Program for Only Women + Minorities. I personally believe that many women and minorities feel this way. I know many white males do.

Educational barriers include professionals who inadvertently add to the marginalization of white males by routinely displaying demographic statistics, mostly showing underrepresentation of and employment barriers to minorities and women. Data should create an open learning environment for all groups; in practice, the data exclude white males. Role-plays in educational sessions may depict white males that have unearned advantages or white-male privilege. White males, according to some training programs, have shielded privilege: they do not have to worry about their race or about getting a job, and they have no clue that they are (still) discriminating if they feel they are not. According to the unconscious bias theory, which has become embedded in diversity as another computer-like virus, white males are discriminating even if they are not, since they are doing it unconsciously! Who makes this judgment? Would you really enjoy experiencing these classes if you were a white male?

Another clearly visible barrier is that minorities and women are significantly overrepresented in the diversity profession. The prevailing thought is that, since white males have the privilege and have never experienced discrimination, only women and minorities should staff diversity and EEO offices. White males in the profession are an anomaly at best. Having women and minorities predominate in these offices is indefensible. It is a barrier of immeasurable proportions and permeates the federal, corporate, and nonprofit arenas—all of which I have worked. Fortune 500 companies, the EEOC, federal agencies, universities, and so forth, still have a majority of minorities and women making up their diversity staffs, which include chief diversity officers, vice presidents of institutional equity, directors of diversity, or of EEO, etc. It is amazing to me that equitable representation is the goal espoused by those who seek inclusion of women and minorities.

How can it be that the same discussion does not include fair and equitable representation of white males? This is an alarming situation. Visibility alone contributes to and supports the white male perception that diversity does not apply to them. How can employers talk the talk but not walk the walk of adequate and fair representation in the diversity offices? Is it that organizational leaders believe that only women and minorities "get it"?

To further illustrate, consider the following example. A company advertises an internal promotional opportunity to a position that is currently and has historically been filled exclusively by white males, stating that they will only consider white males for the position. That scenario, on the surface, would be considered deliberate institutional discrimination. Charges of racism could ensue, and the EEOC would decree that there must be discrimination since a pattern has been established of hiring only white males, to the exclusion of minorities and women. Does this scenario sound familiar? In contrast, white males are underrepresented by percentage of population in the federal government in many agencies including the Department of Veterans Affairs with the exception of the Senior Executive Service (SES).

I am going to take a big leap of faith here and state that there will never be a "special-emphasis" program created to address this issue or any effort whatsoever to hire six or seven more white males, if that was the number of underrepresented in an office. I would assume that diversity and EEO offices should be the beacon in a company or federal agency, but instead they choose to nearly extinguish white male representation. This projects not only marginalization but exclusion to the entire workforce. Having spoken to groups nationwide over the past six years, I am amazed by how many women, minorities, and white males come to me after each session and let me know how great it is to see a white male presenting the training. Why should the diversity profession not take confirmation of this acceptance by minorities and explore how to expand the effort to include white males in this profession?

Surely, as civil rights activists always say about underrepresented minorities and women, "we are out there."

If an EEO complaint were lodged by a white male who was not selected for a position in EEO or diversity, the excuse may be that the applicant was not qualified (even though he was among the best qualified) or there were limited others in the applicant pool. The justification could be a ruse and not supported by facts. It could be a prevailing unconscious bias in their selection, which relies on "optics" and non-selection of white males.

In contrast, let us see if a similar situation in a civilian company or federal contractor was investigated by the EEOC or the OFCCP. Enforcement agencies would consider sanctions or a lawsuit based upon this pattern of institutional discrimination; but not so fast. In instances where it is claimed that there are no minorities and women who applied, the EEOC or OFCCP will say that "qualified minorities and woman are out there, and you just have to find them." But since white males are not a protected category, if the situation were reversed, it would not register. Apparently, these "enforcement" agencies just look the other way if white males are historically underrepresented in the federal government's diversity and EEO offices and passed over for promotion. It is as if the Civil Rights Act does not apply to them. This is a prime example of why white males feel excluded from diversity and EEO and gives rise to their claims of reverse discrimination. Reverse discrimination, of course, does not exist because discrimination is discrimination and can be so for white males because of sex, color and race.

For training purposes, I know I stand out as a white male in the diversity arena. Inherent with the "odd man out" scenario are implicit associations with race. Some participants in sessions may feel that, if the person presenting the material is not a minority or a woman, that person cannot possibly understand the struggle or experience discrimination through employment or education.

These overt associations actually prove that white males are fully marginalized and thought about as a group and not by content of their individual character. I was born and raised in rural Indiana. I experienced what would be considered poverty today and started my working career painting street curbs and hauling garbage before joining the Marines. I could not return to college until fourteen years after high school. Given these humble beginnings, I supposedly do not have a clue what it is to have to struggle and was granted white privilege at birth. I have earned what I have achieved through hard work, grit, sacrifice, despair and success.

I see visual cues for brief moments in my classrooms from those who may feel that it is very unusual for a white male to present a class on diversity. I view their initial curiosity as engaging, leading to connecting with the group and achieving credibility as the class moves forward. The same holds true when I present an LGBT awareness class. I am not LGBT, and some feel that "unless I am one, I should not speak about them," which is a comment I received recently during a class.

If that is the case, then women and minorities, who are the majority of diversity and EEO professionals, would not be able to speak about white males. Is this an illogical opinion? Yes, but inclusion requires respecting someone else's opinion even if you disagree with it. There may be some who feel that I am merely protecting management as a white male (and a member of the white male club). That reaction comes from all backgrounds. Some also may have been dreading attending my course, fearing that they were going to hear my personal advocacy of the extremely uncomfortable "white-male privilege" line.

These same reluctant attendees may also feel that I will, by design, be a liberal and project the white guilt line: that white males need to "get it" and receive revelations of "white guilt" is typically an unspoken objective. Plus, the participants anticipate that I will urge all participants to "get it" like I do! Imagine walking into an audience for the first time realizing that many members of the audience feel like this. There is personal fulfillment of being able to see their perceptions change. Participants are now experiencing something profoundly and positively different than what they have experienced before. Participants appreciate my straight talk and different message of total inclusion, which is quite the opposite of what most have experienced in the past. Hundreds of minorities, women, and white males, who approach me after a presentation or through follow-up e-mails, express how they appreciate that someone like me is a pioneer in this arena and is presenting diversity as it should be. I am really inspired by comments such as: "This is not what I expected; I thought it was going to be the same old diversity stuff" or even "It is about time we saw a white male in this capacity." They are worth their weight in gold, and I will take that feedback over any certificate of appreciation or plaque. White males, merely being in attendance does not equal their participation or guarantee an increase in their diversity awareness or respect for diversity.

Special-Emphasis Programs

Corporate and federal strategic plans are carefully worded to demonstrate their commitment to increasing diversity, removing barriers, and increasing recruitment and representation of women and minorities. White males, however, are virtually extinguished from the same strategic plans and demographic reports. Typically appearing as an inconsequential footnote and with no thought whatsoever of increasing white male "diversity," white males are an afterthought at best. Overall discussion, affirmative action, and any recruitment or retention initiatives have never included white males in the past or present.

Affirmative action plans were developed initially to address underrepresentation of women and minorities. Today, even though women and minorities are overrepresented in many ar-eas, these plans still exist. The reason they still exist, according to those in diversity and EEO offices, is that companies want to make sure it stays that way or that there is historical representation. When will these programs then become history? Another addition to the "long way to go" adage it appears to exist; except we are already there in overrepresented areas of minorities and women. In contrast, if white males are woefully underrepresented, and if statistics showing this are presented to leadership, there is typically a reaction of disbelief. Leaders who previously touted the same report's representative numbers of women and minorities will challenge white male percentages or just shrug and act incredulously like this situation cannot be happening.

Leadership will move on to the more important special-emphasis groups, some of which are very overrepresented, particularly in federal agencies in Washington, DC. Special-emphasis groups representing certain races and ethnicities or women were created to create awareness and address underrepresentation, but they now continue without a purpose—except to exist. Here is a question for your consideration: Who really has the privilege in employment considerations?

There is nearly zero oversight or analysis of special-emphasis programs' return on this investment. Special-emphasis programs are expensive to maintain, but their rationale for existence is never questioned. Special-emphasis programs do not have the ability to directly recruit women or minorities for the federal government or take a single resume, since everyone has to apply on the standard www.usajobs.gov website. Federal employees who are responsible for special-emphasis programs, however, love them. These program managers have the ability to travel throughout the year, attend or host a minority or women's conference at a luxury hotel, and create "partnerships" with women and minority business organizations. Yet making friends has limited impact on the federal government's recruiting efforts; this is only possibly increasing social media contacts.

I have repeatedly expressed my opposition to special-emphasis programs' supposed partnerships. There is never an explanation as to what these partnerships with affinity organizations actually accomplish, other than allowing an organization to publish that it has developed a partnership. The only benefit for the programs is good news for the airline and hotel industries deriving profit from conference attendees. They have only a marginal, if any, impact on diversity awareness or actual recruitment of women and minority applicants. You will rarely see white males attending a conference such as Black in Government (BIG) or the League of United Latin American Citizens (LULAC), etc. I know because I presented cultural awareness training at the 2012 conference at the Detroit Cobo Arena and was delighted to be a part of this, but saw extremely few white males at this conference.

This next issue continues to be a meltdown contributor. There are deep-rooted white-male attitudes and feelings of exclusion with this entire diversity "thing." White males' perceptions and attitudes developed throughout the last thirty years and practically confirmed for most that they are not part of diversity. It was extremely difficult and next to impossible for white males not to have noticed their exclusion. With programs that consistently place them in a less-than-positive light, showing them as biased, discriminatory, or unconscious about their biases and discriminatory behaviors, the resounding message is perfectly clear.

Everyone else is more important than we are, they feel. Sessions with the uncomfortable white-male elephant in the room dictate exclusion or blame, no matter the genuine intent of the instructor. A limited number of diversity professionals, including me, are promoting what true diversity is and stating that it must be inclusive, straightforward yet comfortable. It is extremely rewarding to witness a spark in participants' eyes when they see they are actually included, but at times, it is also difficult to change perceptions. The reality is that current training programs are replicas of past versions of curriculum, which were dreadful to begin with.

Some good could possibly be achieved, even with poor curriculum, but in the end, too much of the "us versus them" theme overwhelms any chance for positive progression of attitudes. I use my curriculum to counter white-male perceptions that it is "only for women and minorities" or "us versus them," and I have had great results. Being a white male in front of them is powerful, but a two-hour class cannot change the attitudes of some who have had a lifetime of faulty programming.

Mainstream programs and initiatives are disconcerting barriers to understanding and acceptance. Well-intentioned colleagues readily accept "new and improved" versions of prior training, but the material remains divisive and ineffective; only now it is disguised. Management consistently searches for a course, any course, that will alleviate employment issues. Employers and educators alike feel there just has to be a magic word or acronym that will achieve greater buy-in from participants and cure all of their workplace ills. New words chosen as replacements remain only as adaptations of diversity, creating even more confusion. When the same things are presented over and over again expecting different results, what does that define? Most of us know the answer. We can break through this barrier by using clarification and reexamining diversity.

Education that separates us will never unite us. Silent codes in presentations trickle through an instructor's facilitation with confusing statistics, graphic representations, special-emphasis and targeted recruitment, mentioning cultural contributions of others—except for white males. How then could "us versus them" be more evident? The theme has to be eliminated—now!

I challenge my classroom participants to reexamine and consider currently held mainstream perceptions, myths, and misconceptions of diversity. I strive to inspire those in my classrooms to feel comfortable and included. Far too many instructors and contractors cling to a curriculum which deliberately makes many attendees (white males) feel uncomfortable as a prerequisite to understanding their feelings. Oh, brother! Would you feel like eating a scone from Starbucks if the person behind the counter told you it would make you sick first and then later you would like it?

That worn-out method is basically used so attendees who do not get it (white males of course) can "get it." What is it that you have not "gotten" during your entire adult life? What a presumptuous phrase! Telling someone to "get it" indicates that they and others already "get it"—except some white males, who are still holding out. An instructor creates an air of sanctimonious superiority that "I get it, and you don't;" it smacks of haughtiness and unjustifiable moral authority.

Instructors or others may say that we need more diversity in leadership or other higher-level positions. You will see many minorities and women in the session nod in approval, but the statement can have another, less-positive translation—and not so many nods. White males, who may quickly scan attendees in the room, will see many of those nods from women and minorities plus other white males with "white guilt." Those without "white guilt" may feel that the nods indicate a more direct statement: "We need more of us and fewer of you in leadership positions." Many white males just turn off with this negative rhetoric directed at them; they endure the uncomfortable classes, play nice, and merely get the box "checked" for attending the class.

These "get it" sessions, whether overt or coded, contain a learning objective to ensure that participants (white males of course) feel "uncomfortable" about their feelings and wake up to historical discrimination, white privilege, or understanding that their biases have gone underground or they are just unconscious about them. There is no specific mention of minorities or women having to experience these feelings, but the way the curriculum is delivered, the message is clear. An instructor will, as they say, push participants out of their comfort zone. Now why would anyone want to do that? Exercises designed to pressure participants into feeling uncomfortable are developed to elicit negative reactions to the point of resisting the class even more. I suppose that "Wow, by golly, I got it" is what they want participants to say or feel!

Some white males will just put on a silent act during the session and play along. Why, then, would any educational objective be to make people feel uncomfortable, resist even more, and drive them to silence? This feeling uncomfortable nonsense still permeates many diversity education presentations. It may be in the form of talking about unconscious bias or some other term, but it is there. Unless curriculum dramatically changes, critical conversations about race, sex, and ethnicity will never be a reality. A difficult dialogue is a far better alternative for understanding than dead silence or ignoring the topics altogether. We all see this as manifesting today with negative attitudes regarding race relations increasing.

Value-added objectives are embedded in my presentations to enhance participants' understanding and help them feel comfortable in the classroom as well as confident and included. The need to feel comfortable with others and respect each other's differences will help create a much more harmonious work environment and overall cultural competencies. I stress that respect does not always equal agreement or celebrating/embracing another person's diverse thoughts, religion, culture, beliefs, sexuality, and so forth. Mutual respect may end at times with just agreeing to disagree and moving on; difference does not equal an inevitable conflict. Those who choose to be engaged with a difficult dialogue, however, will find their own awareness, understanding, and respect of the other person increase.

A new challenge is surfacing. Many educators skip basic diversity awareness altogether. Many educators move directly to more advanced, specialized courses, which amount to intellectual exercises serving only to further perplex participants. Without a basic and genuine understanding of diversity, participants experience even more words and phrases that contain similar false narratives or codes, ensuring that some participants will feel extremely uncomfortable. Educators who are stuck on an "us versus them" way of thinking need not worry; the new, "higher-level" courses keep it, and it is in no danger of being eliminated.

There is not a governing body for diversity education. Employees historically experience classes that are so run of the mill or just plain dull that near zero learning transfer occurs even with "us versus them" themes. By chance, a charismatic presenter may have the talent to make humdrum and dull material fun and/ or exciting (but not educational) at least for brief periods. A carnival huckster can be entertaining too when selling medical potions or enticing people to play a game they cannot win. Both scenarios will fail to achieve desired results or return on investment. While the session with the instructor or huckster may be entertaining, great odds exist for anyone to walk away without anything of learning substance. We need to challenge key considerations of adult learners—not confuse or disparage many of them.

By choosing, year after year, to maintain the status quo, however, employers will not provide a learning experience worth employees' time. Most are missing an enormous window of opportunity for acquiring genuine diversity awareness that would possibly benefit them now and hopefully in the future. Participants experiencing diversity education will continue to misinterpret definitions while the courses maintain the silent but powerful message of "us versus them." Unfortunately, the window of opportunity is closing fast.

Rising rapidly through the tangled web of diversity challenges is the reluctance to even use the word diversity. I keep hearing comments, including, "everyone knows what diversity is, so it is time for something more exciting." Has the sun set on diversity? Are we past the word that no one fully understands? Many also share with me their views that diversity has become passé, and employees have heard enough of it; some speak of diversity "fatigue." They feel the desire to have more desirable words or catchy phrases, such as cultural competency, engagement, emotional intelligence, unconscious bias, and so forth, will inspire and energize employees, since diversity has obviously failed to do so. Leaders who seek out these classes and return armed with these new words will think it is "the last word." Leaders feel that something else is needed. For unknown reasons, there seems to be a compelling need to advance to unproven and still-divisive material that will enable employees to "get it"—but at a higher level! Something more delightful or a term that is more in vogue, they say, will appeal to the masses who will embrace the words, creating harmony; at least, this is their hope; of unicorns and rainbows.

Some of this propaganda is driven by diversity contractors who never seem to run out of words! Many in leadership seemingly seek that miraculous word or phrase that will create "diversified" employees and make all of their workplace ills disappear. Can we all say now we have achieved Nirvana? Right, as if it were that easy.

This unique challenge is perplexing since diversity has acquired so many codes and associations; it has never achieved a definition. Should we extinguish the word in its still-undefined state and prematurely replace it? Many words in the English language evolve, but when the evolution is vague, it is not an acceptable evolution. Consider the word "diversity" as we did before—as a computer that has acquired multiple viruses, distorting everything in the computer. This computer needs the world's best antivirus program to remove existing codes before anyone can even think of moving on to other uncharted territory. Employers may choose new words for expediency, hopeful that the time-consuming "diversity stuff" can be taken care of once and for all. Those who say we have a long way to go are on back roads without a defined end. If they program the precise GPS coordinates (understanding diversity), they can get to the final destination.

CHAPTER 2

White-Male Privilege

When diversity professionals, university professors, and others speak about and actually promote white-male privilege, it literally agitates me. While I do not discount that some of the assertions are based on historical facts, I do discount white-male privilege as an inequality measure today. When does historical become history or does historical always have to resonate as being omnipresent? As a white male who grew up in rural Indiana, I did not have an inside toilet until I was a junior in high school and, believe me, outside toilets were cold undertakings during the wintertime! After graduating high school, even with good grades, I did not have the finances or resources to attend college. There were no minority scholarships waiting for me or someone offering to pay for my college tuition so I joined the United States Marines during Vietnam. I was unable to attend college until fourteen years later.

Not a single person ever gave me a job or hired me because I was white or provided my family with handouts or entitlements. I worked extremely hard to achieve what I have, and I have actually experienced employment discrimination in the diversity profession because I am a white male. Liberals and progressives of all backgrounds take special pleasure in emphasizing what they wholeheartedly believe is "white-male privilege." White males, according to this conviction, have no inkling about what all others, except for white males, experience in their everyday lives. They believe that white males, imbued with this built-in privilege, never have to worry about their race, color, sex, employment, discrimination, education, families, living wages, and so forth. Does anyone truthfully feel that all white males are shielded in some type of protective iron dome fantasy bubble? This is preposterous, but many hold this belief in the existence of white-male privilege and it is acknowledged throughout the diversity world. Most white males will just sit quietly and take it in classes when people start spouting off with this false rhetoric. They make the easier choice—acceding to what they feel is political correctness—and remain quiet. What a shame for diversity education. Their reaction is truly unfortunate but expected, as this is what occurs in most diversity education courses that white males attend.

A discussion of white privilege is rarely a dialogue or the topic of a national conversation. It is clearly and almost always one-sided, and especially lacks input from a conservative thinker like me. This approach in presentations of diversity fully supports "us versus them" themes and perceptions. Stating that no white males have privilege at all would also be incorrect. There can also be black, Hispanic, Asian, Indian, and various other ethnic "privilege" as well. It is only through achieved or bestowed power that one has enhanced privilege. If you took a look at rich people in any nation who have privileges, you would see that poorer people do not have the same privileges. Any race, sex, or ethnicity has equal opportunities to pursue and achieve success. I also realize there are individual dire situations and consequences and choices that doom some to perpetual failure. It takes hard work, dedication, education, and a high measure of resolve to overcome some of life's challenges. Our Declaration of Independence guarantees a right to the pursuit of happiness. Pursuit should not be confused with guaranteed or entitled.

I strongly disagree with what some academics have stated which is that white privilege is perpetual. For example, who actually has privilege in employment these days? There are incalculable programs that benefit minorities and women: special-emphasis, internship programs, targeted recruitment, and affirmative action programs that give preference for the recruiting and hiring of minorities and women with corporations, nonprofits, and federal agencies. These programs continue, even though percentages of women and minorities exceed those of white males in many agencies and corporations. There are inexplicable excuses why these programs still exist. I am told that since the numerical achievement has been accomplished; they want to make sure these percentages remain constant! Take a guess at which group that does not have special-emphasis or targeted recruitment programs? In many cities where there are federal agencies white males are underrepresented by expected percentage. White males are underrepresented in the federal government. Federal contractors to this day must justify hiring a white male rather than a minority or woman for positions they advertise, even if the white male had extensive and overwhelming qualifications and performed the best in interviews. Not having enough minorities and women in the applicant pool sends up red flags to the OFCCP, even if a position is properly advertised and significantly recruited for.

Corporations and federal contractors fear all of these hiring compliance programs and agencies who enforce them. If it is determined by regulatory agencies they did not comply with the outdated perceptions and legal aspects of affirmative action, retribution, court action, and sanctions are swift and can come not only from courts but also through enforcement agencies. These include the Department of Labor, the OFCCP, and the Equal Employment Opportunity Commission.

The bottom line is that power dictates privilege, and individuals should be hired for a job or admitted to higher education based upon merit, not based upon race, sex, or ethnicity. When any person has relevant power, certain privileges will exist—no matter their race or sex. Those who assume that white males, in the twenty-first century, have special privileges no other race, sex, or ethnicity has or can obtain is accepting entitlement versus achievement and also believe in filtered facts. I will challenge this continuing unsuccessful numbers driven mentality in another chapter by recommending the elimination of affirmative action and special-emphasis programs.

The past ten years or so of surveys from Pew Research and Gallup illustrates that a majority of white males feel comfortable with all races, support diversity, and generally have a good impression of the workplace atmosphere. A Washington Post/ABC News Poll conducted July 11-14, 2016, however, portrays a startling contrast with 63% of Americans overall and, specifically 72% of African Americans reporting that race relations are generally bad. The nationwide reaction to the jury decision in Ferguson created a firestorm of racial tension that snapped everyone back to reality. Subsequent tragic events in other major cities increased racial tension in all walks of life without a recourse from history or current ongoing constructive dialogue. Just when white males were adapting to the supposedly effective diversity programs, whites started to express increased pessimism about race relations, compared to previous surveys. In comparison, a previous Wall Street Journal poll published on December 17, 2014 reported unfavorable views of race relations at 58 percent compared with previous survey results of 45 percent. Sixty-eight percent of African Americans in the same poll viewed race relations as unfavorable. I believe this is due in large part to thirty years of deplorable diversity training with an uncomfortable "us versus them" focus and the absence of race relations conversations that Dr. King envisioned and thought would occur.

National conversations on race never materialized after Dr. King's assassination. They were assumed to be too uncomfortable by diversity curriculum designers, who led the way to even more uncomfortable "sensitivity" classes. This path was choosing the easier wrong, as opposed to championing the harder right. Many critical and crucial conversations, which should have occurred during over thirty years of diversity training, have yet to occur. Just like an iceberg, what is not seen is the most dangerous part. We were left with unpleasant training practices in the past that included white males experiencing sensitivity training. They were the ones who needed it, curriculum designers said, since women and minorities already had it or "got it."

On top of that, the sessions purposely included targeting white males with blame, creating exclusion with unconscious bias and microaggressions thrown into the mix. So when white males listen to diversity trainers who espouse white privilege, or they see it mentioned on the news, it's no surprise that there is no overwhelming nod of agreement with that belief. White males basically have had enough and truly want to move on but have to mark time, as they say in the Marines, when the order is given. Women and minorities, it seems, always experience disparate treatment as one measure of discrimination. White males treat them differently, behave differently around them, do not invite them to special events, do not select them for IT positions, i.e., in Silicon Valley, etc. Disparate treatment is accentuated through diversity training, press coverage, social media, social compacts, educational offerings, books, etc. In contrast, major strides in hiring and employment of women and minorities, including substantial leadership gains, have and are occurring. Leadership succession pipelines for both Fortune 500 CEO and federal agency senior executive service positions are increasing in percentages for women and minorities. For example, the US Office of Personnel Management's report released March 31, 2015, highlighted certain demographic trends, particularly with younger women. Women aged twenty-five to thirty-four make up nearly 44 percent of supervisors and managers, versus 35 percent of managers who are aged fifty-five to sixty-four. Astonishingly, there still is near dis-belief regarding many of these positive accomplishments. Why is there an unwillingness by minorities and women to acknowledge profound attitude shifts from white males?

White privilege, it seems to minorities, is still dragging every-one else down—except white males. Women from all races and ethnicities, for example, now achieve more bachelor's, master's, and doctoral degrees in universities, and their attendance exceeds males' by an overwhelming margin; university students are close to sixty percent females versus forty percent males. At what point will someone think that a special-emphasis program for recruit-ing white males to colleges and universities is required? Some women in colleges and universities have actually expressed that they would like to see more men because their campuses do not feel "diverse." Did anyone see this coming?

During my final tour of duty as an Army Major and senior equal opportunity advisor with the Department of Defense Equal Opportunity Institute (DEOMI), there was a course included in the twelve-week curriculum entitled "White Male Privilege." As you can imagine, it was an extremely uncomfortable and de-meaning course for white males. I convinced DEOMI of the over-whelming negative feedback from minorities, women, and white males and was given permission to redesign this course with a different title: Power and Privilege. I have recently confirmed, however, that, while DEOMI maintains the Power and Privilege course title, it clandestinely returned all of the uncomfortable exercises and absurd statements to the curriculum.

Revising and refreshing curriculum is to be expected, but re-inserting false and discarded material from the past is alarming. DEOMI once again is fomenting racial division with this course. They also mention in the Equal Opportunity Advisor Course stu-dent manual the continuing existence of the illusionary "White-Male Club." The manual goes into great detail about this so-called "White-Male Club." An excerpt is below:

"In spite of slave insurrections, civil war, the thirteenth, fourteenth, and fifteenth amendments, the women's suffrage movement leading to the nineteenth amendment, the civil rights movement, urban rebellions and the contemporary feminist movement, the club persists,"

DEOMI Student Manual, 2012.

An End to Whiteness?

Dana Milbank's column in the Washington Post on August 4, 2014, was entitled "End to American Whiteness is Welcomed." With a column that, in part, accused tea party members of defending whiteness, but that did not offer any evidence, Mr. Milbank continues to promote the ideology that any white-male association with whiteness is somehow unacceptable or racist. His column, whether inadvertently or not, in my opinion, slams and ridicules an entire race of people. He also quotes his liberal friend, Eric Liu, who, in his book "A Chinaman's Chance," states: "America has an enduring competitive advantage over China: America makes Chinese-Americans; China does not make American-Chinese." Liu expresses his feelings that what America needs is Chinese values! He calls for "a corrective dose" of Chinese values: mutual responsibility, long-term thinking, humility, moral character, and contribution to society. It's as if he's saying that Americans lack these values and we need to be corrected! I believe that diversity, true diversity takes a significant hit in this and other columns that expose the "us versus them" racial mantra. What chutzpah! Sensational views apparent throughout media sources give the impression or confirm long-held white-male perceptions that white males and diversity and equal employment opportunity (EEO) are not compatible.

Diversity education should be all about us, and we can be truthful and inclusive. Straight talk, no bull approaches to diversity for all adults typically is well-received, with feedback stating that this was not what they were expecting. My participants are not expecting this type of diversity presentation. They have been indoctrinated with mainstream diversity training for most of their professional lives, no matter their generation. Participants realize in my sessions that I do not adhere to mainstream diversity training, which I think is lost somewhere in the Twilight Zone! The atmosphere in my classrooms is an air of inclusiveness and respect both during the training and afterward.

White males should be part of the group leading the charge for inclusion and respect. Barriers discussed in the previous chapter have negated our much-needed presence and participation. There is too much veiled and limited discussion. With crucial conversations and with most diversity educators, exclusion seems to be the order of the day for white males. They are maligned as well as a targeted scapegoat for all of diversity's ills.   There are pioneers who take on this mantle of responsibility and truly espouse the idea that diversity applies to all. Organizational diversity councils in corporations or federal agencies may advocate this sentiment but demonstrate something entirely different with their actions. The person leading the meeting will say that the organization views diversity with a wide brush, yet then go to slides that show where the organization stands on racial and gender demographics and how it must do much better in its diversity. Driven by numbers of racial groups and women or civilian affirmative action plans or the equivalent federal Management Directive 715, the exclusion is formalized in writing.

White males, inexplicably, are not included in this process unless they are listening to the woes of a particular organization's numbers or are responsible for preparing the reports. We are, however, at a point, as will be described in the next chapter, where white males are becoming underrepresented—as shown by those same numbers. What will we do then? I have already encountered those who, at times, appear to be conducting themselves from a higher moral ground and just do not want to confront this scenario, even though it may already exist in their own facility.

I have spoken to and held training with thousands of people in my diversity career. I have to counter perceptions, in every class, what has been so wretchedly presented over the last few decades by other instructors. I fully understand that, as a white male, my mere presence in front of large groups of white males gives me a unique opportunity to unlock deeply held and nearly hardwired associations as well as real or imagined perceptions of diversity. In addition, as a former Marine sergeant and retired Army major, there is additional curiosity about me, which leads people to at least listen and not shut down immediately. When people feel my conservative values permeating the presentation, I believe that my credibility is locked in.

It is very easy to discuss race, politics, religion, generations, and so on with people who are of like mind. It is not, however, as easy in multicultural settings or when a member of a minority presents to a group of nearly all white participants. This would not be the case if the curriculum were inclusive rather than exclusive or if it were designed to help participants feel comfortable about diversity rather than force them to examine their feelings or feel targeted. White males perceive they are the scapegoat and the enemy of minorities and women. Their perceptions are not entirely without historical merit or foundation with the diversity curriculum they encounter. Mr. Milbank's aforementioned "End to American Whiteness" column speaks volumes as well. In another quotation from his column, Mr. Milbank states:

"The United States is experiencing a rapid decoupling of race and nationality: Whiteness has less and less to do with being American." Does being a minority or a woman make you more of an American?

In the last chapter, I stated that nearly all affirmative action plans, diversity strategic plans, recruitment and retention plans, and special-emphasis observance months completely extinguish or eliminate even the mention of white males unless making a direct negative comparison. There is no mention of white male underrepresentation based upon civilian labor force data, no special recruitment or special-emphasis groups to target them; nor are there any white-male-focused conferences scheduled. Therefore, white males see enhanced, progressive, and positive employment actions for everyone else—but not for them.

Many white males in the traditionalist and baby boomer generations (myself included) have experienced firsthand, since the inception of diversity training, painful classrooms where we were taught about "white privilege" and institutional discrimination, which was created and sustained by white males. I was able to at least change one course at DEOMI from "White Privilege" to a much more relevant course entitled "Power and Privilege," which included all races, sexes, and ethnicities.

The *en vogue* term "Unconscious Biases" describes the ways that white males are still prejudiced and exhibit biases even though they feel they don't act, speak, or feel that way. Isn't that belief convenient for those who just cannot get over the feeling of being discriminated against? It appears to me that, if anyone, it is those very same individuals who would have unconscious bias. In unconscious bias awareness classes, the familiar and tired use of the "us versus them" scenarios prevail. In a typical curriculum, there is instruction about how the brain functions and about our hardwired biases. The instructor explains that we can somehow counter these biases by either practicing conscious introspection or awareness or by merely asking others to call us out where they think we demonstrate these biases or discriminatory behaviors.

Anyone who tells me I am biased (due to being unconscious about it or a white male) is simply stating an unproven and unbelievable statement to me. If I am unconscious of something, what person has the medical training, scientific knowledge, or supposed moral authority to tell me that I am unconsciously biased? How do they know what I am not thinking? Will I be told that I am acting out through microaggressions? Where did they get this magical power or intellectual gift? Don't their brains include implicit associations or unconscious biases also? Their observations could simply be their own implicit associations. Or is that restricted to white males? Who can claim the higher moral ground to dictate to others what they may be exhibiting?

Apparently, many heads of tech companies feel that they must attempt something, anything, to drive up their "diversity" numbers. In the July 31, 2015, edition of USA Today, there was an article titled "Pinterest launches diversity project to see what sticks." The title of the article itself supports my contentions: not only has diversity education failed in the past, but companies really don't have a clue. Making something stick is a dangerous strategy for equality. Pinterest co-founder Evan Sharp says the company plans to share what works and what does not so the tech industry at large can learn from the effort. Sinister comments in the article such as, "The statistics are sobering, showing an industry dominated by white and Asian men."

Why is this situation inherently bad, when these employees may be the absolute best? Is the company experiencing a drop in production, research, or creativity and losing profit? Pinterest engineer Tracy Chou stated: "We are not proud of how little our numbers have moved in the right direction." What is the "right" direction? Could it mean "less of you (white and Asian men)" and "more of us (women and other minorities except Asian men)"? When did Asians lose their minority status? It appears that Asian men are victims of their own success—success that included commitment to education, hard work, sacrifice, and drive. That dedication qualified them for jobs that have made many tech companies extremely profitable. Wait, they must have had Asian privilege—but I do not think there is a course on the shelf like that yet! But of course, we have to include our old friend "unconscious bias" in hiring, retention, and recruiting so that highly qualified African Americans, Hispanics, and other racial/ethnic minorities just cannot be hired because white males and in this instance, Asian males just don't like the other groups. Are they for real?

Do you really want this kind of thinking to pervade people's minds like an uncontrollable virus? Well, I suppose since it is stylish and everyone else is doing it—like bell bottoms or disco—businesses and the federal government are hoping this is the new panacea for fixing diversity.

Diversity training organizations constantly churn out new words, terms, and the latest gimmicks to sell to unsuspecting companies or federal agencies that believe that these companies are the "experts" in diversity. I researched one of the "train-the-trainer" courses and found that there were significant omissions, errors, and outright false data and research displayed on the PowerPoint slides and in the study guide. When I conversed with a federal contracting officer, I was told that it was unfortunate that the office that contracted for this content did not review it until after the delivery, so there was nothing to do but accept the product. I wonder how many products the federal government has accepted in this manner. I would hope that other agencies do not have this practice. To give a hypothetical, imagine the FDA, which approves pharmaceuticals. Hopefully they would not approve something only after it is marketed and they witness someone has taken a dose of an experimental drug to see their reactions!

By request, I have had numerous impromptu conversations over the years with white males and minority women and men before and after my classes. These conversations are revealing and include white male reactions to diversity, such as resentment over being frozen out of the diversity conversation or being forced to go to the class. They have stated that they always hear that diversity applies to everyone, but they also hear the message: "We need more diversity." How can I counter these perceptions when they are based in the atmosphere of reality: continual reinforcement of training in this regard and historical factual reference? Many in the classroom basically feel excluded; they are included only through their mandatory participation in these classes.

I reinforce each person's uniqueness and tell them that diversity is all about us and not us versus them. I eliminate these divisive "us versus them" and "white-male privilege" themes entirely. Insisting on this elimination, I have achieved expanded interest and appreciation and generated conversations with all groups, since all groups feel included.

When I present diversity as a concept, I emphasize that each person has primary dimensions of diversity to include race, sex, sexual orientation, physical and mental characteristics, and age. I provide an analogy and use a personal computer as an example, referring to the primary dimensions as a hard drive. Secondary dimensions or software/applications that are added throughout the lifetime enhance that uniqueness of everyone. Secondary dimensions can include areas such as generations, politics, religion, military service, family status, education, geographical location, and so on.

One needs to look no further than the federal government to see how perceptions of exclusion can be real to the white male. In the Department of Veterans Affairs for instance, readily available published figures show that white males make up 23.28 percent of the civilian labor force of the VA, yet according to government-wide representation, they should be at 38.33 percent. Black males, for comparison, make up 7.81 percent of the VA workforce, yet are only 3.7 percent of the relevant civilian labor force which the VA uses for representation. Black females are even higher, with 14.73 percent representation but only 6.5 percent of the relevant civilian labor force.

Blacks, for example, have the federal government's African American Employment Program, required of all federal agencies, along with several other mandated special-emphasis programs. One of the program's stated objectives is "to assist to develop and implement special program initiatives that will enhance the employment and advancement of African Americans." The published VA Diversity and Inclusion Strategic Plan, available online at www.diversity.va.gov, states as one of its three goals "To build a high performing workforce that reflects all segments of society." To the white male, that reflection is not visible in comparison with zero programs or mention of underrepresentation for them. White males then ponder when this will end and when they will be recognized with diversity.

I believe in the concept of diversity, which recognizes that each of us is unique in characteristics, spirit, and beliefs. Diversity is a state of being, always changing yet always around us. As I mentioned previously, the concept, coupled with inclusion, is a powerful workforce dynamic. Inclusion is not a state of being but rather a state of mind where there is consistent learning, sharing, and ability for introspection.

Inclusion is also a recognition that people can evolve from long-held beliefs or perceptions when they fully understand their perceptions or assumptions or those assumptions are revealed to them. Much of what they think may be accurate, but sometimes further exploration and development of cultural competency in areas not explored will lead to a revised conclusion. Inclusion also means that people count and everyone knows they count in the workplace. Many want to belong to something greater than themselves, and with an inclusive environment, the mission becomes more visible and an employee can associate closely with the brand and mission.

President Theodore Roosevelt stated, "Wide differences of opinion in matters of religious, political, and social belief must exist if conscience and intellect alike are not to be stunted, if there is to be room for healthy growth." I believe, as Americans, we all should blend our various cultures and diversity into the fabric of our nation without hyphenating ourselves. I have never referred to myself as a white American or European-American because I am and will forever be an American.

CHAPTER 3

Equal Employment Opportunity

As we continue exploring America's impending diversity meltdown, it will be helpful to review some history, starting with the establishment of equal opportunity laws, emanating from the Civil Rights Act of 1964. Understanding the history that led to the "invention" of diversity is a good place to start. EEO laws were and are necessary to ensure that no discrimination or harassment will occur in the workplace. If these laws are violated, avenues exist to redress this behavior though a formalized complaint process, which the EEOC administers.

American history shows why these laws were created: to protect minorities and women who were historically discriminated against and/or harassed without recourse. Prior to the enactment of the Civil Rights Act and various executive orders, these groups experienced extremely difficult times, facing discrimination in hiring and limited access to educational and promotional opportunities. On March 6, 1961, President John F. Kennedy issued Executive Order 10925, which included a provision that government contractors "take affirmative action to ensure that applicants are employed, and employees are treated during employment, without regard to their race, creed, color, or national origin." This order was followed by a whole host of laws, including the overarching Civil Rights Act of 1964, which addressed employment and education.

Institutional discrimination, however, was already embedded into the workplace. Even when laws were applied, many minorities and women were still behind, due to practices that continued to be followed. Although institutional discrimination is, most of the time, unintentional, many hiring officials continued past practices that resulted in institutionalized discrimination. Job descriptions, for instance, stipulated educational levels that were not needed for the position or demanded many years of experience, which minorities and women would have been unable to achieve. Although these situations continue to be a problem in some areas of the country and in some occupations, job descriptions are now routinely written without unnecessary restrictions or requirements of advanced education or unattainable levels of experience.

In 2014, many people participated in "celebrations" of the fifty-year anniversary of the Civil Rights Act, singing choruses of "We Shall Overcome" and waving signs that read "Unfinished business, then, now, and going forward." My questions are: Who are the "we"? Who exactly has unfinished business? As mentioned in the previous chapter, it appears that the "us versus them" mentality is still very much alive and well. We need more conversation and a little less singing to achieve true equal opportunity. It is important to acknowledge history so we don't repeat it, but moving forward is far more effective than miring ourselves in the past without direction or the proverbial light at the end of the tunnel. We cannot alter the past, but we can dictate the future if we work together.

President Obama's comments, below, regarding the fifty-year celebration offered a mixed message on progress, but the comments perpetuate the "us versus them" theme by mentioning tearing down existing barriers and concealing actually who these barriers apply to. "The Civil Rights Act of 1964 brought us closer to making real the declaration at the heart of our founding—that we are all created equal. But that journey continues. A half a century later, we are still determined to tear down barriers and put opportunity within reach for every American, no matter who they are, what they look like, or where they come from."

When anyone is targeted or made to feel like a scapegoat, a defensive reaction should serve as notice: targeting excludes people. The president's comments emphasized an individual's looks and origin. His own lack of awareness of what diversity is and how it has been presented in the past is truly unfortunate since his words carry so much weight globally. I ask participants in my classes to raise their hands if they have fire extinguishers in their homes or offices. Most in the class raise their hands. I then ask how many have had to use them, and a very few hands may stay up. However, for the majority of people, fire extinguishers, although vitally important for safety purposes or even required for emergencies, are rarely used.

The same limited use of the law should be true now. Fifty years of maintaining a growing list of EEO laws is going overboard. The laws are still necessary, but, in my opinion, the confounding additions to the laws overemphasize and are knee-jerk reactions. As a former EEO investigator, I can attest that many EEO complaints were not valid, some actually were meant to harm the person being charged without merit of the charge, or were used to protect the complainant's position. Many complainants have used the EEO process when it became evident that their time with the company was coming to an end, due to an existing or impending disciplinary action or a falling-out with a supervisor.

Some white males I speak to shared how they or other white males may have experienced "reverse discrimination." I respect their misguided definition of reverse discrimination but took the time to redirect the conversation to EEO law. EEO laws apply to everyone, so there really is no such thing as reverse discrimination—just discrimination—and yes, it does apply to white males. Discrimination by race or color can apply to every race and color—including white males. Since white males have had to sit through all of these targeted and uncomfortable classes, defensive reactions about EEO lead most to feel that the laws do not apply to them.

Many white-male participants ask me when a law will be created that will allow them to file a discrimination complaint. Of course, my answer is that there have always been laws like that, from the beginning of civil rights—laws that protect them. The looks of astonished disbelief are profound but understandable. Their reactions are similar to looking at someone who is awakened from hypnosis. Yet, discrimination, when referring to racial discrimination, is discrimination. Discrimination can occur, regardless of a person's race or color, and it can even be within the same race. Many white males I speak with have not been told that white males are included and protected in all categories of EEO and can file a complaint if discriminated against or sexually harassed. That is simply astounding, since we have had these laws now for, what did we say earlier? Fifty years! Do thousands of EEO trainers nationwide inadvertently disregard or not mention these facts? The messaging or training is not clear at all for white males. As a white male, I am able to file an EEO complaint against another white male or against a minority and/or a woman, including charges of sexual harassment, as long as my complaint meets the criteria of a valid EEO complaint.

A valid (not proven) complaint consists of one of the protected categories of Title VII (and EEOC guidance) to include, race, age (over forty), sex (including identity and pregnancy), color, national origin, genetics, religion, retaliation for current or prior EEO activity, and disability. The complaint must also include an employment action, such as denial of promotion, retaliation for filing a complaint, dismissal, creating a hostile working environment, and so forth. Both criteria have to exist for an EEO complaint to trigger an investigation. What is not commonly known is that the EEO process is supposed to protect both the complainant and the respondent to the complaint.

I know that people from all races, sexes, and ethnicities continue to suffer from discrimination and harassment. This is because there are some small pockets of pure hatred and ignorance within every race in this country and the world for that matter. What I am contending, however, is that EEO as a program has not evolved and is still operating from the perspectives and attitudes of the sixties, seventies or eighties. Stopped in time like a broken watch, the EEOC acts as a vindictive, rogue enforcement agency, not as one in which all parties are protected. Their unwritten motto is "litigate first, investigate later," and they have been vilified by the courts for not applying the law as it should.

In addition, EEO investigators are, as are diversity professionals, overwhelmingly minorities and women. Since neither of these professions project fairness in their own makeup, it appears that the investigators are merely advocates for the individual complainant. What if all or most all of the investigators were white? This profession cannot appear to be fair so long as the majority of investigators, even if they are fair and equitable, are members of races and genders that do not reflect society. It is vital that an EEO investigator maintain objectivity and protect the process, which is to apply the laws equally, protecting both parties and the process. Unfortunately, many feel a compulsion to take on the advocate's role rather than doing what they are required to do which is to protect the equitable administration of the process for all parties involved.

EEO professionals must contend with laborious documents, such as affirmative action plans or their equivalent, the vaunted Management Directive 715 of the federal government agencies. These serve no useful purpose except to meet reporting requirements or to identify "barriers" to employment. Hardly anyone reads these monster documents, except for the EEOC, and they have the effect of limiting EEOC's ability to achieve equal opportunity. Affirmative action plans typically contain a workforce analysis, position groupings, identification of "barriers," and requirements that the company undertake what the Office for Federal Contract Compliance calls "good-faith efforts," to ensure equal employment opportunity.

The federal government's affirmative action equivalent, Management Directive 715, has similar requirements to identify "barriers" to employment for minorities and women. These so-called barriers are not fully explained, except that when a certain minority (again not white males) is underrepresented, based on comparison with the relevant civilian labor force, a barrier must exist. It must exist, even if that "barrier" is analyzed and found to not actually be a barrier. That is just not good enough. A reason must be there; a barrier does exist only because the "numbers" say so or because their unfounded interpretations of the data say so.

An agency has to perform a "drill down" analysis to go deeper into the data, whatever that means, to find something, anything, to which to attribute the underrepresentation. Even if they cannot find a reason, after this "drilling," they must still report underrepresentation of whatever category of minority or woman as a barrier.

Google, Microsoft, Cisco, and other tech companies are repeatedly challenged regarding their "diversity." These companies, and many others, finally announced that they wanted to improve upon their diversity (code for increasing numbers of blacks, women, and Hispanics—not Asians or white males). These companies did all of the "right things" stating it was the "right thing to do," saying it would increase productivity and enhance decision-making, pouring massive amounts of capital into diversity programs. They did this even though they are some of the most highly successful companies the world has ever known—with their existing "numbers." Even so, they announced that they were continuing the "improvement" of their diversity. Fewer white males and Asian males in the workforce was the improvement they were masking behind that statement of improvement.

Time headlined a June 1, 2015, online article with the tired phrase: "Google's Workplace Diversity Still Has a Long Way to Go." Again, there was no mention of the reasons for Google's lack of diversity. Activists asserted that there were minorities and women "out there" with qualifications. They must be way out there because even with a massive recruitment effort, applicant pools to reflect their version of diversity was not significantly increased. What was also not mentioned is that people who might have basic qualifications might not meet the standards of extremely highly qualified individuals or graduates of top universities.

Significant retraining of individuals would have to occur, as well as retrofitting of university curriculum in technical areas to qualify individuals who graduate from institutions with substandard technical or scientific programs that do not match requirements of these leading tech companies. Should it be the responsibility of successful companies to address, pay for, and achieve this magical diversity equality? Or, should universities and colleges with substandard curriculum in technical fields hold themselves accountable? It is their responsibility to prepare students to achieve success, so they should meet twenty-first-century standards. Lowering standards in companies to achieve diversity does nothing for productivity, innovation, or profit, but pressure from special-emphasis groups is driving more of the change than ever.

It is perplexing that, according to both affirmative action and M-715 plans, an unfounded barrier (which is a barrier that cannot be evident or proven by bias or discrimination) is still one, even if no qualified minority applicants applied for the position! I consistently hear from civil rights activists when they are confronted with the fact that no minority applied that "they are out there, and we just have to find them." Another caveat is that a barrier exists even if there were no minority or female employees available in the agency already in the succession pipeline for the position advertised.

The unproven yet prevailing thought is that a potential minority or woman applicant simply did not know of the position or where to look for it, or was not in the pipeline for some nefarious reason. Unfortunately, these types of artificial and unbelievable barriers are used to justify continuing special recruitment programs for every "underrepresented" minority group, even if they are not still underrepresented. We have to cast the net wider, as these programs announce, or simply find underrepresented minorities and women, wherever they may be. It would appear that minority and women recruiters and civil rights activists believe that, other than white males, women and minorities are sitting at home, reading only minority publications, or they just don't have a clue where to apply. Candidly, if I were a woman or a minority, I believe I would consider the above beliefs to be an affront to my intelligence.

For federal employment, someone just has to direct these underrepresented groups to the only online site that lists positions for the federal government. The federal government, which maintains a federally funded special-emphasis recruitment program dedicated to doing just that, is absurd! Apparently, only white males know where to look for jobs in federal government since they do not have one of these programs for them. I will let everyone in on that secret website and it is www.usajobs.gov. Nearly all jobs for the federal government are on that site and everyone who wants to apply for a job with the federal government needs to go to the site, create and account and submit their resume. Since white males have never had a dedicated special-emphasis recruitment program to show them where to look for positions or how to get promoted, they must have superior intelligence and inherently know about all of this employment stuff. It is either that or total exclusion, hoping that white males do not know and will not apply.

The next challenge is those who refuse to believe the representation numbers they see popping up in many locations, which show that white males are actually "underrepresented," based upon numbers in the relevant civilian labor force. I was at an institution recently where the numbers shown to a director clearly demonstrated that black women and men were actually overrepresented by a considerable margin, and white males were underrepresented by a large percentage. That director stated that he did not believe the figures. This is so, even though he had stated previously in the presentation how proud the institution was of the improvement in its "diversity" over the years—based on the same numbers in the report! The demographic pendulum is swinging; white males are becoming underrepresented in many employment areas. Nearly all who are in the diversity profession are being caught off guard when presented with this dilemma. Yet, they do nothing and do not even know what to do. Confirming diversity education's failure, even diversity leaders have been so thoroughly indoctrinated with white guilt that it is unfathomable for them to now support white male diversity equality. Oh, how the pendulum has swung the other way.

I have attempted for years to argue that the time will come when we may have to shift our recruitment focus if equality becomes unbalanced. If we are going to have "special-emphasis" recruitment programs for everyone but white males to enhance representation in underrepresentation, what will we do when white males are shown to be underrepresented? All I typically receive is a shrug or comment that it surely will not happen. That is an alarming reaction, since it would then appear to most that it does not matter. Or, as I suspect, many believe that white males were the majority for so long that it is okay for them to be a minority, without the need to recruit more for a while, so we can still say we have a long way to go! I am not a betting person, but it would be long Las Vegas odds to think that a special-emphasis recruitment program for white males will be developed anytime soon.

CHAPTER 4

Perspectives

What does diversity of perspectives or individual thoughts actually mean? Literally, it is the unique thoughts and beliefs that each individual contributes to a conversation, decision, or recommendation. Most diversity educators, when discussing diversity, usually express that diversity is not all about race, sex, or ethnicity, but also about diversity of thought. That is a nice sentiment in theory, yet in actual practice, it is just not the case when the majority of people equate diversity with just race, sex, and ethnicity. Why? The answers are relatively simple.

Driving diversity throughout most employment or human resources circles is the demographic "proof" that they are doing what they are supposed to be doing in terms of racial and gender representation. Federal government agencies and federal contractors, for example, are mandated to show that they have special-emphasis programs, reports, affirmative action plans, and so on, that are structured with measureable data, particularly numbers and percentages of minorities and women, which are captured and reported in the laborious reports mentioned earlier.

While it may be desirable for companies or agencies to actually use these reports in productive ways, it is impossible to measure such things as diversity of thought, religions, politics, socio-economic status, or a whole host of other categories that comprise true diversity. Military, LGBT, or disability status, for instance, can be measured only if that information is volunteered. Diversity of thought or perspective is not discussed even with diversity professionals. Therefore, the subject of diversity continues to be influenced by people who are not reflective of society as a whole in this country. A primary example, as mentioned in previous chapters, is in the diversity and EEO profession. Since its inception, the overwhelming majority of diversity or EEO professionals have been women and minorities. White males like me are clearly a distinct minority, visible only if we are truly pioneers and out front with leadership. Those who wish to complain about a lack of diversity due to demographic representation should look no further than at this profession.

Scrutiny of the profession does not occur, however, since the perception by minorities, many women, and white males alike is that diversity is a program for minorities and women. Perceptions have not changed since the inception of diversity programs. So how, with extremely unequal racial demographics, could there be diversity of thought driving diversity education? While some minority and white-male life experiences may be similar, most have not been compared. These perceptions are brought into the training arenas by mostly well-meaning minorities and women, and, by extension, to the diversity profession. The resulting lack of diversity of perception has relegated the diversity profession to stagnation of ideas while perpetuating clearly outdated diversity philosophies.

The obvious disparity of representation of races, ethnicities, and sexes in the profession creates confusion among those instructed. It creates perception barriers for educators like me who, in genuine earnest, try to counter those perceptions. Everyone is diverse, and everyone has unique qualities. Diversity is truly a broad spectrum of differences not relegated to race, sex, and ethnicity. The profession itself, however, reflects a much different mosaic. It practically confirms what many white males are silently thinking. Since they feel excluded, they choose not to be a part of the discussion.

Some in the diversity profession came from other professions, such as human resources; others, unfortunately, have been assigned to diversity out of necessity and without prior training. I would not like this to be the case for other professions, such as, let's say, the medical profession, mechanics, police, firefighters, or the military.

Diversity of thought depends upon those in the diversity profession who have had experience, situational learning sessions, and discussions in the field and younger generations mentored by other diversity professionals to be given the opportunity to promote what diversity truly means. Those in the diversity profession just accept the current ideology, based on the past, without question. The result is the impending meltdown.

Since the majority of diversity professionals are women and minorities, I witness agreement in the profession on a whole host of veiled diversity rhetoric. Typically, it is what would be considered on the political spectrum to be very liberal and victim-based. I think of the Fox News show "Outnumbered" at times, since I am outnumbered myself twenty-five to one in my own diversity and inclusion office. Everyone basically respects me and the work I do nationally, so when I offer a counter to near-unanimous agreement on a topic, some people actually speak up and agree with me. Those are the conversations that we need to have in diverse groups. We must have more who have the courage to speak up, take on political correctness, and experience what may be uncomfortable but also crucial conversations. Most choose not to offer their opinions and remain silent. I refuse to remain silent, and while I am sometimes called a maverick, I also hear remarks from thousands of people who enjoy my presentations and their content. Evaluations have been outstanding from facilities nationwide. This type of validation from grassroots employees and leadership alike tells me I am on the right track with my epic challenges. I hope that I will eventually open the floodgates to diverse opinions of white males who do not suffer from white guilt—and even those who do.

Diversity of thought can be stifled by those who wish only to perpetuate the past and cast minorities as victims incapable of knowing where to seek jobs, promotional opportunities, or career advice. Diversity of thought can also be a major challenge when those thoughts are contradictory. We consistently hear from everyone involved with diversity that differences are our strength, different voices make better solutions, and so on. What we must understand, however, is that too many differences in a group can cause as many problems as it solves, depending on the culture. When everyone's trying to work together, finding a common platform can be a challenge. A culturally diverse workforce has potential strength in its ability to make valuable recommendations or complete projects efficiently. However, being culturally diverse, the different views and perspectives sometimes can contribute to solution gaps, ongoing frustrations, analysis paralysis, and conflict. Overcoming these obstacles can be challenging but not impossible when one is comfortable with and open to differences.

"We are all different, which is great because we are all unique. Without diversity, life would be very boring."

Catherine Pulsifer

One method is to increase the cultural competencies of individuals so they can appreciate the thoughts and conversations of others who are different. Cultural differences take on many forms. Similar to diversity, culture is often defined as a person's particular cultural (or country) heritage. The definition must extend to regional cultures as well, which contain their own unique cultural factors.

Secondary dimensions of diversity discussed earlier in the book, such as generational, religious, political, parental, or educational, can mean that people are more or less deferential to authority or have greater or lesser degrees of autonomy in the workplace, which can differ from a company's needs. Differences can cause reactions ranging from collegial to caustic. Finding common ground requires a high level of psychological safety, which allows open exchange that respects the perspectives of others. We must be able to realize and respond to these differences.

Political Correctness

We can see the collective anger over political correctness in Donald Trump's campaign for president. Somehow, his challenges to political correctness are resonating with all demographics, as if they have been silenced for quite some time. Mr. Trump is the Republican nominee and has been successful, because so many of us are PC-fatigued! As children, we soak up established, existing values from the surrounding culture, values so prevalent that they are rarely challenged or questioned. Exposure to additional ideas and beliefs can happen through indoctrination (where students are taught what to think) or education (where students are taught how to think), or we can learn through our own curiosity and questions.

Regrettably, ideas and moral values are challenged by political correctness, which places freedom of speech on the run from the heat-seeking missiles directed by PC adherents. Free speech is targeted by those who feel that absolute political correctness should be the norm for conversations. Doing so restrains speech limiting any chance for a productive dialogue. Those who jump on every word someone uses as politically incorrect want to live in a protected bubble of comfort, without fear of anyone saying anything bad. Relinquishing any ability to have straight talk, we are relegated at times to speaking only niceties or trying to mask a word with a hyphen or use a euphemism to be safe. Normal conversation experiences these artificial barriers, which are based upon the oversensitivity of a few people who may be offended by the use of a word, phrase, or designator. Do we really want to continue this downward spiral of politically correct speech? Or would most prefer straight talk and the truth revealed in critical but respectful conversations? Our country was founded upon the ability to counter arguments, which can sometimes be heated, even when respect is present. We witness this behavior now on college campuses, where students are demanding to feel comfortable in some type of safety zone of non-harmful speech. Yet, sequestering free speech is adding volumes to the diversity meltdown, both on campuses and throughout our society.

Political correctness now has a growing number of hyphenated words which undermine and confuse while requiring a person to carefully choose these hyphenated words from a separate dictionary in their minds. The fact remains that even though we may say a hyphenated word to be politically correct, the real word still registers in our minds and there are a lot of restrictive feelings that go along with it for the other person being spoken to as well. Take the N-word for example. This word still resonates in a person's mind, and we hear it—only silently. The word is enhanced by its full use in music lyrics and in some blacks' conversations. Other races tend to be non-pejorative in their language, so as not to offend. Is not the use of the hyphen word still offensive in the company of others in employment environments even if we are intending to not offend?

One can readily witness the nervousness, absolute confusion, and dismay of those who do not wish to use a certain word yet hear others freely use it. Some might listen to songs that contain a particular word, hear people singing along—then be told by those same individuals that they do not have a "right" to use that word. What right are they referring to? If a word is a term of endearment to one race or ethnicity, how can it be discriminatory or inflammatory when another race uses it in the same way?

Who actually has the moral authority to assign a word to the scrap heap of the politically incorrect dictionary? Words cannot be simply hyphenated out of usage but are being allowed to be extinguished due to fear of not being politically correct. Words are either banished to footnote status in the annals of communicative history or allowed to be used colloquially. Excessively calculated PC conversations contribute to what I term "impending conversational implosion," so as not to offend anyone. Surely we do not wish to offend or be harsh to anyone, but sometimes offending speech comes only after a crisis—and then from those who have been offended by perceptions and assumptions that arose in the crisis. Free speech has been regulated to the corner. That is not a good omen for America's diversity but another contributor to a meltdown.

More and more expressions are being labeled as "hate speech." What convenient labeling for those who do not want to engage in what could be a productive conversation. Hate is a supercharged, emotional word that no one wants to encounter. Adding "hate" to a conversation shuts down those who never had hate to begin with, but are silently or verbally accused of it. When hate is spoken, it immediately requires adjusted speech and adherence to PC language. One now has banished an increasing number of inappropriate words to the proverbial PC dictionary or risk the wrath of the opposition if they are used in conversation.

How can a discussion of diversity be initiated without those who act sanctimonious and refuse to engage in productive conversations? The phenomenon of oversensitivity is growing, and crucial conversations are decreasing. The outcome has quelled any other viewpoint, which has led to diverting attention from acknowledging diverse views and facilitating racial relations to the non-progressive, PC environment of the status quo.

In the next chapter, we will continue the discussion of non-PC writing by providing a challenge to an evolutionary topic. I would like for you to consider how "communities of color" or a community of a certain ethnicity or religion can or cannot contribute to diversity. In my opinion, communities of color are the embodiment of chosen divisiveness and exclusion.

CHAPTER 5

Communities of Color

As discussed previously, diversity continues to absorb inexplicable meanings or attributions. Self-proclaimed communities of color or communities of specific ethnicities or religions use labels that are not fully defined or understood. "Community of color" labels unfortunately contribute to diversity's confusing meaning, purpose, and, yes, its meltdown. These communities themselves encompass preconceived attributions about others that may or may not apply. Do these communities actually exist as they are labeled and with the attributes assigned? Senator Rand Paul, on September 30, 2014, stated: "We need to reach out to people where they are ... We need to be more diverse and look more like the American people. The message has to be broadened to reach more people."

First of all, what do these communities actually mean or represent? Of course, Senator Paul, in his speech, is referring to the Republican Party, but too many times, we are stuck with such phrases as "reflective of the community" or the black, Hispanic, Muslim, Jewish, or Asian community, neighborhood, or voters. Do these communities all think the same way? Is everyone in the community in lockstep or as lemmings, driven to the same conclusions or destination? What is reflective of white people?

What about members of these "communities" who have conservative viewpoints or do not wish to be lumped in together as a "community?" Are whites, who surely live in some of these communities, excluded from the discussion, since they may be a minority? The challenge is clearly evident in my view. There is a lack of common sense if Americans believe that communities of color should exist in our republic. Communities of color, by their very design, are to be considered set apart from the rest of the community, thus perpetuating exclusion. The concept or reality is flawed and divisive, not only in appearance but in practice. Driven by media and highlighted stories that contribute to altered states of awareness, communities of color, and so forth, are never thought of in true diversity but perpetuate "us versus them." For instance, when Senator Paul states that we need to look more like the American people, is he including or eliminating white in that statement? You can see how this may be off-putting to people who are white—unless they feel they are part of his "American people."

Alignment with a community of color creates division and perpetuates "us versus them." Some of the very same people who fought for Dr. King's dream of content of character versus color of skin are now aligning themselves to the color of their skin. So many in the original civil rights movement abhorred this alignment and wanted to change; now they want to change back? What are they thinking? This retro mentality actually translates to "us versus white males" or whites in general, and it is devastating to diversity. I realize that in most inner cities, there are neighborhoods comprised of mostly one race or another or possibly a concentration of a certain religion. Those in the media, however, and in the communities themselves, attribute their beliefs about an entire race to historical concepts of victimhood or individuals' inability to make up their own minds. That portrayal should be an insult to everyone of that race. Trying to tap into the votes of an entire community may be prudent in those communities where people have historically, and with little reason, voted for the Democratic Party, since they are worse off than when President Obama took over nearly eight years ago. Repeatedly, we see situations where it seems that every race, ethnicity, and gender in this country is unable to deviate from what is expected of them—except for whites, who seem to be the only ones capable of making up their own minds. I do not believe it is the absolute truth, but so many in communities of color carry misdirected anger and even hate toward whites and especially white cops.

White males do live in these same communities of color but are the minority. Yet, unlike their neighbors of different races, white males, it seems, are free to choose to be liberal, conservative, libertarian, independent, etc. White males are also able to live in or beside these "communities," or in any other part of the country of their choosing. It seems that referring to the white-male vote or a white community is immediately translated as a reference to racism, white power, privilege—well, you get the picture. Nerves are really frayed from all sides, and diversity is melting down.

All others in communities of color must be victims or unable to succeed in our diverse society because of white males. A community of color actually translates to a code in these "communities" for combating racism and victimhood and thus enhancing "us versus them." It is impossible not to divide rather than include, for interests are self-serving to a particular race, ethnicity, or religion. Those in the "communities" who choose to deviate from what is expected of them (such as being conservative) are ostracized, criticized, or just plain extinguished from participation in the community. A "community of color," then, would appear to be any color other than white, and it absolutely would not include white males. Where is the desire for race-relations dialogue and not confrontation?

General Mills has a well-intentioned grant program, the "Celebrating Communities of Color Grant." The grants are open to nonprofits, including schools, theaters, and other Twin Cities organizations with programs that support people of color. While this is a worthwhile corporate social-responsibility program and has helped many, the continued use of "communities of color" is "us versus them" or giving to anyone but whites. Let's get this straight. If you are a white person living in a supposed community of color, are you able to obtain a grant? Why use code? The website clearly states that the program was established ten years ago in recognition of the foundation's fiftieth anniversary and aligns with General Mills' commitment to diversity, which is a company core value and a key business strategy.

Does General Mills' program show a true commitment to diversity? My challenge here, as with other well-intentioned programs, is that it specifically targets "people of color," which actually excludes—even with philanthropic intentions. General Mills' commitment to diversity is to increase its involvement with people of color—except for the color white. Therefore, its commitment to diversity is exclusive and goes against the grain of true diversity. General Mills, and others of well-intentioned like mind, seek to have employees who reflect the "community"—while never mentioning that diversity also includes whites or white males. Unintentional hypocrisy drives companies that acquiesce to "communities of color" for monetary reasons. Throughout my career in diversity, I have encountered many colleagues who buy into the philosophy that most all minorities and women are underprivileged, underserved, or undermined. Thereby when "communities of color" are mentioned, these attributes immediately apply to them. Some of my colleagues may acknowledge, when I bring it to their attention, that the black middle class has grown dramatically. They merely overlook that, stating that we still have "a long way to go," which is a typical response, spoken as if it were on a teleprompter.

Cultural competency development with diversity considers many relevant factors that have a direct affect, either positively or negatively, on cultures or races. Yet these factors are rarely if ever discussed in diversity presentations. It is as though such important factors as family structure, education, legal status, and generations, are not relevant somehow to the concept of being underprivileged. Underprivileged, by definition, means not enjoying the same standard of living or rights as the majority of people in a society. For instance, black married-couple families earn more than twice that of single black female-headed households, but seventy percent of births by blacks are to single parents; this factor alone substantially drives down income. Choices made by those in communities of color to drop out of school and have children out of wedlock do have life consequences; yet they seem to have expectations of entitlement and a standard of living similar or equal to those who made different and more productive choices; such as those who stayed in school, worked hard, and are married. Regarding single parents, this is not a judgment against those who become single parents but the less desirable outcomes of single parenthood are the facts.

It is not a matter of being underprivileged; it is a matter of having a cultural variance that does not compare favorably with the results of choices made by others in this country. If a person makes personal choices, some may be the result of current circumstances. Yet, there are too many resources that exist for that same person to claim being underprivileged is the underlying factor for lack of opportunities or motivation. Perpetuation of poverty as a result of personal choices is not an excuse either. History alone cannot be a permanent excuse for failures or desire to succeed.

The second claim, that of being underserved, is also a very contentious one. It is known without a doubt that the more education a person has, the more he or she will earn over a lifetime. Many blame the poor school systems, but the counterculture of not wanting to learn is more to blame than the school systems themselves. Disciplinary actions have skyrocketed in inner city schools in communities of color. Why have they not in outlying school systems? Teachers are just as committed but must endure, in spite of attitudes of many students that prevent learning. We need more Joe Clarks (*Lean on Me*) to run schools and rid schools of caustic behaviors—not cater to them.

The latest report on the statistics of college graduates states that Asian Americans have the highest rate of completing college, with 60 percent obtaining a bachelor's degree. Forty percent of white Americans have earned a bachelor's degree, compared with 23 percent for blacks and 15 percent for Hispanics. How does being underserved apply here? Asian Americans have a long history that demands educational excellence in order to be successful. White Americans have had that same resolve but have dropped dramatically over the last decade, and the Black/Hispanic completion rate clearly demonstrates a lack of resolve in comparison. Blacks and Hispanics are not excluded from schools or colleges but make choices that lead to their exclusion. I know that there are other socio-economic factors involved with college completion rates. Blacks, for instance, have a sixty-three percent graduation rate from high school. This factor alone creates a large swath of the population ineligible for the labor force beyond menial jobs. Many black women become part of the 70 percent statistic of single parents and perpetuate a reality of lower income, without means to escape. Many programs exist, but many choose not to participate. The Hispanic population has other challenges besides having only a 15 percent graduation rate in college. Challenges are not because of being underserved but align with relevant factors, i.e., lack of English proficiency and lack of parental support at home for high school, due to parents being illiterate, possibly illegal and having a severe lack of English proficiency, or just not being capable of assisting their children in school. Communities of color that harbor individuals in this category must instill the will in others in their community to learn English and the will to succeed.

I coached girls' soccer for many years and finished my soccer coaching career with the last two years at a high school with a very large Hispanic population. One of my additional duties as a varsity coach was to provide counseling and work out a plan to help when a girl had difficulty in school or was getting a bad grade. I spoke with one girl of Hispanic heritage when I was informed by the school guidance counselor through an academic report that she was failing Spanish. I knew that she spoke Spanish very fluently and asked her how she could be failing this subject. She stated that, while she could speak Spanish, her parents were illiterate, illegal immigrants, and unable to help her with such things as conjugation and sentence structure. We worked out a tutoring arrangement, and she eventually passed with good grades, but you can see how this was a cultural factor—not being underserved. Programs existed for her parents in the high school to assist them but they did not want to take advantage of those programs. Rather it was another cultural variance based upon the choice of parents to immigrate to a country without the skills to speak the language, assimilate into the culture or assist their children to learn the new language. I knew her parents and they were in this country for over fifteen years and never learned the English language; choosing only to speak a broken English which did not allow them to participate with volunteer activities at school. How could they help their daughter, if their will to learn was not there and they did not assimilate into American culture?

My personal feeling is that it should not be the "Hispanic community" allowing lower school standards when there is an aversion to learning English and not being able to fully contribute to their children's education; this sets up failure in college. Nor should these same Hispanics claim they are underserved as an excuse for what might have been a poor personal choice or setting their children up for failure without any means to assist. There are federal and state programs that use taxpayer dollars to provide specialized language services; it is the law according to Title VI of the Civil Rights Act and Executive Order 13166. These can be successful, but it takes a tremendous amount of work, and, as we see from the statistics, this does not bode well for college completion for Hispanics.

Undermined is another perpetual theme that is almost always associated with women and communities of color. The true, guilt-laden liberal and progressive mindset, when using the term "undermined," probably can recite the actual definition, which is to attack by indirect, secret, or underhand means or attempt to subvert by stealth. Their objective is to create white guilt to drive funding to communities of color. It does not matter that all Americans have rights under the Civil Rights Act of 1964 and myriad other equal employment opportunity laws and policies with protections for an increasing number of people, religions, and mental or physical conditions.

There are still many professionals and others associated with the diversity arena who believe that people (white males) are not discriminating overtly now, but covertly! I feel that their view is disheartening. Seriously, I think they imagine white people who go home at night and dream of ways to discriminate against someone without being caught. These same people probably also envision the white males in white sheet robes with pointed hats posing in front of a mirror each morning before work!

New terminology, which continues to permeate communities of color, includes additions to the words "discrimination" and "bias." One such term is unconscious bias. For some inexplicable reason, unconscious bias is the optimum and *en vogue* word that minorities and women and minorities feel good about hearing— but many also do not feel applies to them. Who is the culprit? You guessed it: the white male. Although white males are not specifically mentioned in the unconscious bias training, it is unspoken but it is assumed and understood by those in the audiences of diversity educators. "Us versus them" is as strong as ever, with sides depicting the way white men view women, minorities, selections, and so forth. We all have implicit associations, of course; our human bodies are influenced by the reactive portions of our brain, which is programmed for survival. However, repackaging material with new terms like unconscious bias or microaggressions is just like re-gifting. It is still the same present, only for another unsuspecting person in another type of gift wrapping paper, who will either toss it or give it to someone else. Communities of color? We need just to be communities of Americans. Until we do, it will always be us versus them.

Gateway to Race Relations World Cafe

Using the World Cafe method of interactive conversational dialogue created by Juanita Brown and David Isaacs in 1995, I launched the first federal national conversation on race with the US Department of Veterans Affairs with over forty volunteers of the Records Management Center (RMC) on April 28, 2016. The title of the session was "Gateway to Race Relations Dialogue World Cafe" and it was a resounding success. What better location to start than in St. Louis? Volunteers who made history that day included black residents of Ferguson, Missouri who were employees of the RMC along with members of many other races. The dialogue was respectful, productive, and open which allowed for free flow of communication amongst races. The same profound results have occurred in successive events in Philadelphia and St. Louis VA Regional Offices with other major cities VA facilities including Portland, Oregon and Detroit, Michigan on tap for September 2016. The World Cafe method is an energizing and engaging dialogue that allows for cross pollination of ideas leading to solutions. Through the use of questions that matter, participants explore areas outside of the relegated politically correct arena. All of the written evaluations regarding the experience of participants were profoundly positive.

It was an exhilarating experience for everyone in attendance. It proves that together, we can break down the "us versus them" and instead replace it with an "it is all about us" mentality. This type of dialogue can help reverse America's diversity meltdown but the dialogue must grow throughout the country and in many locations. Following Dr. King's lead, doing what is right is not easy but necessary. We cannot allow the current state of race relations to fester to unrecoverable levels.

CHAPTER 6

Identities

"In this country, we have no place for hyphenated Americans."

Many Americans require an ethnic or racial or sexual identity association of some type. How each citizen or non-citizen identifies himself or herself creates an immediate identity. As with communities of color, without a hyphen or group identity, many in this country would feel left out and without an identity. Hyphenation of identities by race, religion, and ethnicity categories has to be politically correct. People will always use their country, religion, or ethnic origin first with their identity and then American. Starting from African, Hispanic, Native American, Chinese, Japanese, Indian, Vietnamese, Korean, Mexican, etc., the lists go on ad infinitum. The same identity association holds true with religion, where we see Muslim, Jewish, Buddhist, Hindu, and so forth. Sexual identity has also quickly inserted itself into conversations, where a person's racial identity might be overshadowed by identity as a member of one of the LGBT categories, for instance.

Identity is part of our conversation. What it means to be diverse and inclusive in a workplace or community is not to have people who look different, but to create an environment where people feel like, at the end of the day, they are who they are. Most people feel the need to find a way that integrates them and dislike feeling trapped in a box; identity, it seems, gives them a way out of the box.

We're going to have to find a way to talk about diversity that isn't just about categories but is about the kind of organizations we want to create for people. Everyone should be able to bring their whole self to work and be whole people without reliance on identity hyphens.

The number of words people use to describe themselves can be overwhelming, but it's important to recognize that these words are often part of a closely held identity. I support associating and honoring your heritage, religion, sexuality, and heritage. Substantial historical context is involved here in the necessity for certain groups such as black, Asian, Hispanic, LGBT, and members of different religions to bring relevant issues to the table and discuss historical discrimination. The discussions, hopefully, can end some discrimination that still occurs. In areas such as housing, employment, and education, discrimination still affects limited portions of the country. The larger issue is not race or heritage but individuals taking responsibility for their actions.

The government is only able to stretch or create so many dollars before the crush of debt stops the treasury presses. Far too many also feel entitled. They contend that they still experience the historical effects of slavery or bigotry from long ago. Some need to consider a major redirection of blame or excuses here because so many other factors are involved, such as personal choices, family status, education, and motivation. The only entitlements we are granted in the Declaration of Independence are life, liberty, and the pursuit of happiness. Many feel that the "pursuit of happiness" must be given to them without pursuit in their personal circumstance. This pursuit depends upon effort or initiative; others who achieve happiness find their own way and utilize their talents. Which way would you feel is the most equitable and fair path for all Americans?

Identity divisiveness occurs when an individual places his or her heritage or religion first in a hyphenated identity. When someone, for example, identifies as a Hispanic American or Jewish American instead of American Hispanic or American Jewish, it immediately places that person into a category of not only being different but also making that more important than being American. How should a white person in America identify? Of course, there are those of Italian, Irish, German, English, or French descent, but there are very few among them who would identify their heritage first. Rather, they would just state, if asked, that they are Americans with a certain heritage or history. An expectation for minority groups to identify and form communities with like-minded individuals has evolved into divisions, created barriers, led to assumptions about others, and created bitterness toward other groups, mainly whites.

Every politician routinely seeks the black, Hispanic, Jewish, or LGBT vote as a bloc, so to speak. They feel as if these "communities" vote pretty much in lockstep with their leadership. No one ever says they want, although they need, the white vote, since they know, even though there are base groups of each party, that most white-voters in the end make up their own minds. I believe we should eliminate the hyphen—or at least have an identity that appears secondary to being an American. Those who feel compelled to identify as hyphenated Americans, please try placing your other identity after American. You may feel more like an American and part of the culture, thus achieving the American dream by assimilation—not by separation or entitlement.

How can we achieve true diversity and maintain inclusion in America when there are those who choose to separate and identify themselves first by race, ethnicity, religion, or sexual orientation versus simply as Americans? It is, by the way, all about us as Americans. To further illustrate this point, a group that calls itself Black Lives Matter believes that it is racist to have an opposing view or to add that Black Lives Matter but White Lives Matter and All Lives Matter as well. The former governor of Maryland, Martin O'Malley, found that out during a recent campaign appearance in July 2015, when he received a vehement reaction; the vitriol continued and was so great that he actually apologized for saying what he said. Why? Don't white lives and all lives matter? His sudden retreat from a radical and racist activist group founded conveniently upon a false narrative shows that Governor O'Malley was not ready to be a president, and he eventually withdrew his candidacy. I have read many of the statements of the leadership of Black Lives Matter to gain insight. I do agree with Black Lives Matter on one major point. They are bringing back to life difficult conversations that went underground and have remained dormant for decades. There is always some, even if limited, common ground to possibly build upon. Inclusion of differences does not mean acceptance of the other's beliefs; one may acknowledge and respect another's views even in disagreement. Hyphenated groups and their leaders sometimes make unnecessary, destructive, and counterproductive statements that only confuse and infuriate fellow Americans.

Women have made progress, but LGBT individuals have not come as far yet with their acceptance in the workplace or in educational settings. Today, women make up about 60 percent of the college and university population, achieving more bachelor's, master's, and doctorate degrees than men; women star in top-rated television shows in lead roles; and women are in all occupations. They have also achieved great success in business, especially by creating a talent pipeline leading to even greater leadership roles in the corporate and federal arenas, and many are now CEOs. Technology has provided many women with increased opportunities for work-life balance, but the workplace has also significantly reduced other women's significant roles, such as the role they have in nurturing children and their much-needed psychological presence in the family.

I am known nationally in the Department of Veteran Affairs as an ally and champion for LGBT awareness, protections, and acknowledgement of gay marriage. LGBT identity was an area where it was necessary to increase awareness and to achieve equality in many areas, including employment, housing, education, and marital status for members of this group. Sometimes the need for change has to be considered, even if the change is not always acceptable to others. The courts, however, prematurely decided the marriage issue, instead of the people, and finally the Supreme Court settled it.

A significant percentage of Americans, approximately 35 percent to 40 percent, according to polls taken in 2015, indicate they are still opposed to gay marriage. LGBT activist groups vehemently state that if you are opposed to gay marriage you must be anti-gay. My discussions with VA employees across the country indicate that this is just not the case; people are just adhering to their religious beliefs about the term "marriage." Many have no qualms about civil unions. Isn't it curious that one word (marriage) can cause even well-intentioned people on both sides to harbor confrontational disagreement? In some instances, and with deeply held religious beliefs, that is certainly the case, but most people are accepting and caring people in this country and just want to allow equality for others.

LGBT individuals and all Americans have witnessed the gradual changes from "Don't Ask, Don't Tell" in the military to the lifting of the ban for gay servicemen, to allowing them to serve openly in the military. Transgender individuals are now allowed to serve as well. Americans who are Gay can now get married throughout the country. These "advances" also contribute to the diversity meltdown because these changes have happened too quickly for some and without majority approval of American citizens. We are currently going through such mandated laws and presidential directives that address bathroom rights for transgender students and employees. In my opinion, it certainly would have been preferable to have had a national referendum on these matters during the next election cycle. It would have then become evident that either the majority of Americans supported gay marriage or the right of transgender individuals to use the bathroom of their gender identity or they did not support either issue. Instead, many relied upon polls and created significant divisions of the population with LGBT hardliner activists resorting to name-calling and disparaging remarks to those who disagreed. President Obama and the Department of Justice also acquiesced basically stating that granting bathroom rights was the right thing to do and comparing their decision to African Americans as another example of civil rights. Morality judgments of a few have resulted in angry responses, boycotts of companies such as Target in 2016 who stated that customers of both sexes can use either sex's dressing rooms of one's choosing, and there are lawsuits arising from states who refuse to comply. Would not a referendum and a national consensus either way served the American people better? The jury is still literally out on these issues.

In addition, court actions did not take into account the deeply held religious beliefs of many Americans. Instead, these beliefs were and are still dismissed as being anti-gay, homophobic, or out of the mainstream. There are estimates that over 100 million Americans still oppose gay marriage. These Americans beliefs and views were not respected by many in the LGBT population or by the courts. Instead, courts felt compelled to overturn constitutional amendments in several states; eventually the Supreme Court agreed with those courts. What is ironic is that an increasing number of people in this country supported gay marriage and had favorable opinions of LGBT individuals through increased awareness until these issues were forced upon them prematurely.

Because of increasing awareness of and association with people's lesbian and gay identities, many non-LGBT individuals are becoming at least somewhat familiar with the terms gay and lesbian, as well as bisexual. In a disturbing colloquial twist, some LGBT individuals use words that have a negative connotation, such as queer, dyke, or fag.

LGBT individuals may consider themselves to have "reclaimed" those words, but it is important for those who are not LGBT to ask what words to use to when speaking to a person who identify as LGBT, out of respect. In addition, individuals who identify as LGBT should realize the historical indignation associated with certain words and be careful when using them in front of others. It may cause confusion and enhance already embedded stereotypes. No one has a "right" or moral high ground to use demeaning words, regardless of claim and exclude others from using the same words. All Americans should eliminate demeaning words entirely from their vocabulary if they are harmful words. One group or another cannot merely own or reclaim these harmful words exclusively for their enjoyment or use; that is nonsense.

It is interesting that our younger generation in the workforce, for instance, infused a "don't care" attitude about sexual orientation into the mix; eventually, they would have muted any existing law themselves, simply through their attitude. We cannot, however, change the way so many other people believe or think—but we also cannot describe them as hate-mongers. And that includes individuals identifying as either lesbian, gay, bisexual or transgender.

Sexual identity will stay with us, but we must also proceed with caution, understanding all viewpoints and accepting tolerance. Yes, tolerance, since no one has to accept the deeply held viewpoints of another, but tolerance fuels respect in the end. As of this writing, we still find that LGBT identity and gay marriage are issues that still contribute greatly to America's diversity meltdown.

Religious Identity

Religious diversity increases the range of moral values and provides perspective on the prevailing values in each belief community. This broad range of belief and knowledge, religious and secular, becomes part of a diverse marketplace of ideas. An intimate part of a person's identity may be his or her religion. What a person believes internally should be a positive contributor to American diversity. It has become, however, an unfortunate and unwitting partner to the diversity meltdown as well. Our nation includes members of all of the major world religions.

I try to conduct my life by the "Golden Rule." While this term is the Christian version of rules of conduct found in the New Testament of the Bible, other religions throughout history have had their own versions of this expectation of followers' human treatment of others. Some individuals who adhere to no religion or to other spiritual beliefs also maintain civilized standards of conduct with expectations of being treated similarly. Everyone has some form of ingrained behavioral code. Many try to adhere to it throughout their lives, whether they are atheists, agnostics, humanists, or members of a religion or spirituality. Unfortunately, there are also those who live by standards of conduct that are aligned to their interpretation of a religion, which is harmful; ISIS and al Qaeda come to mind.

Religious identity is very personal for those with deeply held convictions; it actually can be a culture all of its own. Religious identity can also be less deeply held by some, for instance, those whose religious interpretations are based on social status, belonging, and comfort or just being around others of like mind. Increasingly, more people are becoming either non-religious or unaffiliated, contributing to a subculture of religion; a recent Pew Research Poll refers to this category as "nones."

"Nones" are individuals who might have held religious convictions from their youth, but who choose not to be aligned and no longer hold those convictions. Religious individuals with deeply held beliefs can suffer from strident, bitter, and personal attacks based on another person's preconceived and unlearned view of that religion. Our nation has constitutional protection from establishment of any one religion and the freedom to express any religion we choose. This freedom extends to both belonging to and being able to disparage a religion through free speech. But there are expectations of integrity; we should all act in ways that reflect our highest moral principles—and that includes civility—this should prevent boorish behavior toward others. Many times it does not.

Muslims in America, for example, have to endure assumptions and associations about their religion, including disparaging remarks. These views are understandable to a degree, since the news media report on the never-ending terrorist attacks by Muslim extremists around the world nearly every day. How could one not form implicit associations with Islam and terror? It is not being bigoted but realizing the way things are right now.

Even though the majority of Muslims do not accept any form of terrorism, the memories of 9/11, the recent brutality of ISIS, the Paris, Orlando, and San Bernardino radical Islamic terrorist murders and millions of refugees fleeing Islamic terror, etc., are etched in most Americans' minds. It is not unconscious bias but conscious reality. Islam does not support any form of sexual orientation other than straight—and absolutely no gay marriage. Gay sexual orientation, if discovered, carries harsh penalties in Muslim countries, which prohibit homosexual behavior. The deplorable treatment of and lack of status for women in many Muslim countries adds to the negative associations believed by others outside the Muslim religion. Yet other affinity groups that supposedly support women's rights and equality in this country remain silent. Can anyone say political correctness?

American evangelical Christians from some denominations experience, at times, vicious personal attacks from LGBT activists, due to their opposition to gay marriage. Evangelicals have deeply held religious beliefs that a marriage should only be between a man and a woman. Catholicism has absorbed condemnation from advocacy groups because of the sexual abuse scandals that were covered up for decades.

Americans who are Jewish are under attack in many parts of this country by hate groups and opposition groups of Palestinians, Iran, etc. Religious identity is a major driver of values in America and can be an extremely diverse positive aspect. It is, however, rapidly becoming an unfortunate added ingredient to the melting pot created by others outside of religion.

It is not our differences that immobilize us but the silence or inability to challenge others who place blame and ridicule on others. America was founded upon religious freedom, principles and values, and unless we maintain them, there will be a major shift in attitudes, caring, empathy, and honor. It seems that nearly everyone cannot engage in genuine religious debate without fear of offending others. Most people avoid conflict or cannot accept rejection of their religious beliefs or have zero tolerance of another religion. With regard to those who champion free speech and straight talk, one cannot muster passion all of the time while being limited to only what sounds nice to others; human beings were not built to be perpetual volcanoes. On the other hand, there are those on the sidelines who need to get into the arena with me to save the freedoms we still have and prevent a diversity meltdown. Remaining on the sidelines is not an option anymore; for anyone.

Legal Status

Legal status, or, rather, the number of people in our country without legal status, has reached critical mass and is melting down our diversity. The United States is supposed to be a nation of laws. Unfortunately, not all laws are enforced. American citizens are told by many illegal immigrant groups and our own Department of Homeland Security to look the other way, ignore the law, and be totally fine with allowing others to break it. Homeland Security states that they will only deport illegal immigrants who are felons. How will they determine who is a felon when these people cross the border? Ask them? Both illegal immigrant activist groups and Homeland Security state emphatically the people coming to the USA are hard-working and do the jobs Americans do not want to do. This assertion supercharges activist groups. American citizens witness millions of illegal immigrants entering the United States and know that it affects our culture. For anyone to view this otherwise is a mistake beyond any proportion. With a massive influx of people from countries illegally entering America each year, the actual count is incalculable; there are estimated to be between 12 and 20 million in this country.

According to a Pew Research Poll from November 2014, Mexicans still make up about half of all unauthorized immigrants (52 percent), though their numbers have been declining. Asians are actually the largest group of new unauthorized immigrants in America, surpassing Mexicans. Most come legally, with student or other visas, and just stay; they become illegal by not adhering to America's limited invitation to come and visit, study, or work.

Each year, the Border Patrol apprehends hundreds of thousands of aliens who flagrantly violate our nation's laws by unlawfully crossing U.S. borders. Illegal entry without documentation is a misdemeanor, and, if repeated after being deported, becomes punishable as a felony. It is supposed to be a good news story now to hear that there are a few thousand less illegal entries into the United States. That is akin to saying that your nearly fatal wound is not bleeding as much now, but you will not be able to stop it, and you will die anyway—only a little later.

Illegal immigrant groups, and even affinity associations that espouse racial animus, like La Rasa (The Race), are hard-core activists who feel entitled and support those who break American laws. Organizations like La Rasa and others highlight only niceties about all illegal immigrants, as if any group of people would be so generalized. They state that America is a nation of immigrants, which is true, but immigration of the past was legal and people assimilated who came to this country. Their arguments get weaker when other facts are mentioned. One-third of all federal prison inmates were unauthorized when apprehended. Many crimes are committed by thousands of illegal immigrants, including murder, rape, robbery, drugs, etc. So much for the statement that we hear so often which is that *all* illegal immigrants *are* hardworking and do not pose a threat. An American who believes that anyone coming into our country must be legal is not racist or bigoted. We do, however, want our culture and border protected—as any other nation does. We welcome immigrants who wish to become Americans but not those who only come for benefits of citizenship without becoming a citizen.

I mentioned earlier a girl on my soccer team whose illegal parents could not help with her homework. According to the Pew Research Center report released November 19, 2015, about 7 percent of K-12 students had at least one unauthorized immigrant parent nationwide, but some states, such as California, at 13.2 percent; Texas, at 13.1 percent; and Arizona, at 11 percent, have substantially more, which means more resources are required for educational programs, funding for school breakfasts/lunches, etc.

Gangs have increased exponentially with illegal entries, with MS-13 and other cartel-like gangs controlling large swaths of major cities and striking daily fear into other illegal and legal residents. Border security proponents like me have been likened to racists and nationalists and never viewed by activist groups as just wanting security in our country supported by enforcement of existing laws. Their shortsightedness and support of lawbreaking is increasing the chances of a meltdown.

Driving through many neighborhoods in this country, I can clearly see that illegal immigrants are the majority, especially in California. On a recent trip to present training I made a wrong turn and when I asked for directions at a gas station or ordered food at a McDonald's in Southern California, I found that no English was spoken and menus were in Spanish. Our melting pot is melting down because of those who come to this country not wanting to contribute to American society and just maintain their own identity, without assimilating. By this I mean by learning the language, obeying the laws, and not feeling entitled to receive every benefit reserved for American citizens without earning it. One can come to this country legally and contribute to the diverse culture—with the objective of becoming an American and being part of our culture. The fruit bowl versus melting pot theory is indefensible; it is clearly not working, it never has in history, and it never will.

No other country in the world has as porous a border as ours. Illegal immigration activists and identity groups try to force their will upon our education, social structure, employment, etc., as if the illegal immigrants are somehow entitled to these things. Europeans are experiencing this now with the massive influx of hundreds of thousands of "refugees." European cultures are being diluted, and their way of life is affected by those who do not understand or want to understand those cultures. Many refugees, as we have seen, have terrorist ties and create harrowing atmospheres both in Europe and here in the United States. Immigration is one thing, and people who come to this country legally are welcomed with open arms—legally. Those who do not come legally should not be welcomed and should be returned, but cities in our country flout laws without repercussions.

Sanctuary cities contribute to America's diversity meltdown. Sanctuary cities whose leaders ignore laws that they feel are harmful to illegal immigrants and refuse to cooperate with federal officials should be held accountable and sanctioned. I am not sure how the leaders in those cities can live with themselves. Just look at the recent murder of a young woman in San Francisco by an illegal immigrant who had been deported five times! What do you think would happen to an American who immigrated to another country, such as Russia, China, or Japan, for instance, and demanded that the school system print everything in English, provide the children with free breakfast and free lunch, and demanded that country's equivalent of food stamps, while paying no taxes to boot? Well the boot would be on you know what; that American would be on the way back to the border or on a plane ride back to America. There would be no "six strikes and you are out." One strike will do anywhere else in the world.

Some diversity professionals display their own bias. They lecture about coded racism in those who lack support for welfare or concerns about undocumented immigration and national security. How can it be racism for someone to believe that welfare should be only for the truly needy and used as a safety net, not as an occupation, expectation, or entitlement for those incorrectly termed underprivileged? How is it racism when we want our own border laws enforced? Those who espouse this higher moral ground are showboating being morally superior to other people rather than respecting the views of the majority of Americans.

I discussed earlier how special-emphasis programs are a waste of taxpayer dollars in federal agencies. The government actually contributes to this through special-emphasis recruitment programs for Hispanics. Every agency does a "barrier" analysis to figure out why Hispanics are not represented in numbers similar to their population in the United States. What most people in our country do not realize is that the Census Bureau counts everyone, regardless of legal status. Its website states, in response to one of the frequently asked questions:

> **Do the data on the foreign-born collected by the Census Bureau include unauthorized immigrants?**
>
> Yes. The U.S. Census Bureau collects data from all foreign-born who participate in its censuses and surveys, regardless of legal status. Thus,

unauthorized migrants are implicitly included in
Census Bureau estimates of the total foreign-born
population, although it is not possible to tabulate
separate estimates of unauthorized migrants.

Identities, understandably matter to people, but they should
not matter as much as being an American and a legal American.
Millions of people from all heritages have sacrificed during our
history so other legal entrants into our country can enjoy the
freedoms we have. The United States is still the envy of all others
in the world. There are no boat flotillas of people leaving America
for another promised land or people crashing the wall at our
southern border to get back into Mexico or to their countries in
Central and South America.

For those who choose to immigrate to America, it just has
to be through legal means. For those here illegally, if they are to
stay and wish to retain a portion of their heritage, they certainly
should be able to do. They also need to work hard to be assimilated, so they can refer to themselves as American first and then
hyphenate whatever they want on the right side of the American
identity. That is not racist but just good old American pride in
our country.

CHAPTER 7

Rhetoric

Flaming rhetoric is a perpetual battering ram contributing to America's impending diversity meltdown. We hear the term rhetoric a lot, and rhetoric by definition is language designed to have a persuasive or impressive effect on its audience, but it is often regarded as lacking in sincerity or meaningful content. Rhetoric and repetition so many times take the place of hard evidence. Self-appointed civil rights activists, some of whom worked with Dr. King, clearly are not representing the will of their own people. Dr. King worked so hard so that others could become self-sufficient—proud of their heritage but also judged by the content of their character. Where is the justice in these civil rights activists' deliberate actions to do otherwise? They are charlatans, and their racially charged rhetoric is what is commonly referred to as race-baiting. Many of these civil rights leaders prey upon the emotions of others during a crisis. Yet they are admired by many in the minority communities, and some are welcomed in the White House, even though they may owe millions in taxes.

Always visible and enhancing or creating hate from those who would riot, disparage, and foment violence rather than work to achieve racial harmony, their messages create nothing but discord.

Previous chapters in this book described the various "us versus them" themes these so-called civil rights activists and leaders of the movement continue to use to inflame by their intentional rhetoric. There are many reasons why people follow them, but their reasoning in my opinion is clouded by failure to acknowledge responsibility.

Rather than acknowledge bad choices they have made, i.e., not finishing school, abusing or distributing drugs, being part of gang violence, single parenthood, incarceration, etc., some would rather blame someone else. These topics have to be part of any discussion of race, ethnicity, or religion. Rhetoric is a perfect word for those who, unwittingly or not, are wrecking the foundations of diversity for their financial gain, victimhood status, etc., rather than being a model for achieving a post-racial world where equality is an expectation and not a destination.

Immigration activist Jose Antonio Vargas, in his MTV short documentary, *White People*, corroborates my premise of how white males particularly were left out of the diversity curriculum and discussion. Vargas said, "I don't think we can have those conversations about diversity and not include white people in the conversation. For me, that's why I wanted to make a film that is centered on unpacking what white identity is and what whiteness is, which for me is such treacherous territory."

Vargas is an activist who wants to dismantle whiteness, is apprehensive about what reactions will be if whites are included, and believes whites are an institution, not a race, in America. His remark about treacherous territory is as if all whites were members of the KKK or Aryan Nations. They are not. Surveys over the past decade, reveal that the majority of white males have had no problem with what they felt were improving racial relations. Unfortunately, due to the fragile nature of race relations, those survey results have pushed the needle to the negative in more recent surveys. The Ferguson, Missouri, and Baltimore, Maryland, riots of 2014 and 2015, with other incidents of police shootings of unarmed black men, shifted attitudes to a much more negative posture. It was as if there was a caldera beneath the surface ready to explode. Political correctness masks the true intentions or feelings of women and minorities; these feelings are only brought out in anonymous surveys or through an atmosphere where people feel comfortable with each other and can have productive dialogue.

Underground apprehension and prejudice on the part of many minorities and women is precarious. Dormant issues, just like a dormant volcano, are pressurized and volatile. The issues did not become extinct. Dormant issues essentially permeate the atmosphere. This drove inclusion of white males to the farthest corners of their minds when they developed the initial diversity curricula. What white male would want to go into that dangerous territory, knowing how minorities felt? A minority or a woman would feel comfortable only when on the attack. Deliberately placing white males in a defensive posture has resulted in silencing them in what should be constructive dialogue amongst all races. Exclusion of white males, except in disparaging them in diversity training, is alive and well, only it's better hidden.

Check to Checkmate

Diversity activists seem to actually enjoy agitating and relying on excuses, rather than finding solutions. In Daria Roithmayr's 2014 book *Reproducing Racism: How Everyday Choices Lock In White Advantage,* her view of "us versus them" is at the forefront. She writes that there is a "lock-in" of racism that whites perpetuate and reproduce based on their historical and current "privileges." Racial cartels from the Jim Crow era, which controlled housing, politics, employment, and wealth, are all still active, according to her theory. Activists like Ms. Roithmayr believe that the system is so "locked-in" against minorities that it creates an attitude of "why bother," particularly with the black population.

Yes, why bother to educate yourself, strive to increase your socio-economic status, escape from poverty and/or low income housing, or apply yourself to excel when you get a job? No one expects anything of you anyway, so why bother? Those who choose this self-fulfilling destiny are making a personal choice. They claim they are now entitled due to their personal locked-in status—an excuse Jose Vargas would love. Visualize, as some activists state, being handed a lifetime sentence in a maximum security prison at birth, without any hope of parole or release. Maybe you could if you were born in a terrorist state and had to live under oppressive laws. Being born in America, however, grants a myriad of freedoms, employment and education programs. Even if you were born into poverty, there are ways to pursue your dreams. Sure, it is tough to get out of bad neighborhoods or a rough family situation. It can be done and it is hard; yet bad choices are made throughout this country by those who feel locked-in. It is a well-known fact that the percentage of blacks with a college education who are imprisoned is a fraction of that of non-college-educated blacks. In response to this statistic, Thomas Sowell stated in his syndicated column on February 22, 2016, "Does the above mean white cops check out the education of blacks before they decide to arrest them?"

Recent court decisions repeatedly state that unyielding racial quotas are not justified where discrimination is not proven. Activists believe, however, that the courts should consider their flawed "locked-in" theory when making decisions. I am very pleased that courts do not do this (yet) because belief in "locked-in" status is becoming the most bitter ingredient in the impending meltdown. Interestingly enough, the same activists who argue for "locked-in" also disparage those who take the Harvard Implicit Association Test (IAT). The IAT's purpose is to measure an individual's biases associated with whites, Asians, and even most blacks. Activists feel that everyone uses stereotypes, is unconscious about it—and should also take into consideration blacks being locked-in to their environment! Blacks, they feel, are an anomaly when compared to other races, which must be "locked-in" to some other dimension.

My colleagues question why I feel so strongly that diversity is in a nuclear meltdown stage. Diversity (or more rightfully stated, racial) activists believe that racial inequality is automatic and continues, even in the absence of intentional discrimination. I feel that I started a friendly chess game already in a "checked" position. I, for one, do not like to be one move away from checkmate. Locked-in? Maybe, but I can choose to leave the game and play with someone else or play another game.

I certainly cannot argue that American history has not played a part in past and present discriminatory practices and behaviors commonly referred to as institutional discrimination. I taught this subject as a race relations instructor at the Department of Defense Equal Opportunity Management Institute for over four years. A concerted effort by business and government to correct these institutional barriers has removed many of these barriers over the past fifteen years, and significant progress has been made. Institutional barriers still exist, but they are being minimized by committed individuals who want to ensure equal opportunity for everyone.

Fifty years of Equal Employment Opportunity laws; creation of special-emphasis programs; affirmative action plans for any federal contractor having over fifty employees and monitored by the Office for Federal Contract Compliance have all contributed to a compliance versus inclusion based system. Then there is the short-fused, rogue Equal Employment Opportunity Commission, which will litigate a complaint without probable cause or investigation and has been cited by the courts for doing this. These agencies and associated special recruitment programs for minorities and women all demonstrate overenthusiastic actions without regard to their effectiveness or accountability. In addition to the above, civil rights activists will not be satisfied with anything short of income redistribution which will magically breakdown the barrier of "locked-in." Unfortunately, money is not the answer but hard work, determination, resilience, and determination to succeed just might be.

Astonishingly, activists claim that minority schools are not as adequately funded as "white schools". This claim is easily debunked. The latest 2015 figures from the Census data reported May 2015 show that the dreadful schools in Washington, DC, receive the third-highest amount of federal funding in the country, at an average of nearly $18,000 per student, compared to Utah, with an average $8,000 per student and significantly higher graduation rates. A glaring example is Camden, NJ, which is 50 percent black, 15 percent white, and was declared as recently as 2008 to be the most dangerous city in the country. It receives $23,350 per student and has a 38.6 percent graduation rate. There is proof right before activists' eyes, but they keep spouting falsehoods to support their not-so-hidden agendas.

American Values Under Siege

Why do our American values resonate with most Americans and others around the world? Although not specifically defined as such, most Americans would agree that freedom, democracy, religious or spiritual beliefs, hard work, empathy, strength, honor, hope, life, liberty, pursuit of happiness, and love of family are some that are permanent values. Messages, advertisements, and the like focus on values that strike a patriotic chord with real Americans. The pride we feel when we see an ad for the few, the proud, the Marines echoes the pride of the present and pride of the past. For those of you who do not feel a tear (or several like me) while watching a value.org commercial, I suggest checking your pulse.

Our values and associated emotions are part of our diversity in America and the magnificent people who form our great nation. We are, however, experiencing "death by a thousand cuts" through the methodical transformation of our country and its values. Major negative changes are occurring both slowly and suddenly at times. Unfortunately, it has been through mounting wounds that cannot be healed without reversing course. These wounds, if really revealed to Americans in total, would be perceived and proven to be as objectionable and unacceptable by any measure of reason. Members of the greatest generation from World War II can only shake their heads in disbelief at what is now happening with the millennial generation, the first in our history which will do less well than the previous generation. Even though we have congressional representatives, the profound transformational changes dictated by the signature of presidential executive order or judicial decision overrides the will of the American people in many facets of our lives ranging from healthcare, marriage, immigration, and taxes to name a few. Even though both houses of Congress are controlled by Republicans, they sit back and do nothing to stop it. They are complicit in their actions through their callous disregard for the American people.

I am fighting back through my book to awaken people from their apathy to our diversity or to American values, both which are melting down. The special interests of a few have overcome unexpected non-challenges from the silent majority, merely by shouting them down. The majority of the majority, it appears, would rather listen to intolerable music and experience unwanted change rather than facing the music and shutting it off. Far too many Americans are restrained from the fight and retreat. That reaction is not the pride and strength of our diversity. Watching our military be dismantled right before our eyes, to the point where Marines will have to catch a lift on an Italian ship to storm beaches, should be anathema to Americans. It is to this former Marine.

Our Veterans have witnessed the near-dissolution of the Department of Veterans Affairs for years. They have had to endure inadequate treatment, tragic waits for claims processing, and employees who demonstrated inept and sometimes criminal behavior who still remain on the job without accountability. Alarm bells did sound for some, but the claxon should be ringing constantly until this situation is corrected for the most diverse segment of our population. We already have to catch a lift to the space station from the Russians, since we no longer launch manned vehicles ourselves. Instead, NASA claims that fighting global warming is its new mission! Enough is enough!

What could have been thousands of years of creative and innovative advancement for America's diversity has been "checked" by multiple incursions of attacks by those who would rather destroy American values and create whatever utopia they have in mind. We can still be the best and retain our American values, but time is running short, and the meltdown is primed to begin—if it has not already arrived. Only one more move to reach or avoid checkmate!

CHAPTER 8

Guardians of Peers

The military, by design, relies upon standards of conduct that demand both loyalty to the service department the member belongs to and compliance with the Uniform Code of Military Justice, which applies to all service men and women. Officers and enlisted service members alike rely on each other, establishing a deep trust that may not be challenged because their lives might depend upon it. As an enlisted Marine and then as an officer in the Army, I experienced diversity working at its best.

Within the ranks, there are service members from every part of the country representing every race, color, or ethnic background, religion; all politics; people from rural, urban, and suburban areas. People from farm country, suburban and inner-city residents, both young and old, all are serving a cause greater than themselves; all with a wide range of fantastic uniqueness.

My first military encounter, on the yellow footprints at the Marine Corps boot camp in San Diego, was a jump-start toward unity and strength. That harrowing hundred-day experience of creating a Marine created in all of us a bond that lasts a lifetime. Although primary dimensions of diversity were visible, these seemed to pale in importance or meaning. Even more interesting were the secondary dimensions of diversity of each individual, such as their abilities, religion, family status, military education, where they served, etc.

Reliance on each other was a given, and the pride in the unit and mission was paramount. I realized there were also unsatisfactory military members whose conduct was not honorable and whose performance was less than stellar. Later, as a commanding officer of a unit, I experienced a mere handful of these soldiers and officers, compared to the overwhelming majority of service members who were honorable, hard-working, and passionate men and women.

What is unique about the unsatisfactory performers is that they typically were dealt with by their own peers—the guardians of the unit who served with distinction. We served with like mind and were one in such regard, as we felt the honor and pride of serving our country and would not let anyone act differently without addressing it. The concept of Guardians of Peers can be of great benefit to the further development of what true diversity should be.

The real barriers to diversity, however, exist in those programs, policies, special-emphasis, affirmative action plans, etc., that seek to divide rather than to include. Within the Department of Veterans Affairs, there are over 100,000 military veterans who work in all facilities throughout the nation; comprising over 30 percent of the employees including senior leadership of the VA. These numbers are astonishing to me due the embedded values that are within each Veteran. Veteran core values. should have compelled these employees, above all, to immediately pursue complaints and revelations and stop illegalities and incompetence. This crisis could have been prevented with leaders acting with integrity. Non action by leadership served to nearly bring down the VA. Instead, many chose to take or acquiesce with other non-veteran employees to steer clear of confrontation versus doing what would have been the harder right. Some did do just that but not enough to stop the crisis and veterans having to experience tragic wait times for treatment. It is a fact, published through the Office of Special Council, that, as of this writing, the Department of Veterans Affairs has the most whistle-blower complaints of any federal agency, including the Department of Defense, which has twice the number of employees. One must realize that whistleblowing is often a last resort for employees. In most cases, it occurs when a problem has been brought to the attention of someone who should have taken action but did not.

Our embedded military values do not depart the day we are discharged or retire from the service. All of the military services echo the supposed values of the VA, which are integrity, commitment, advocacy, respect, and excellence (ICARE). Yet many veterans allowed the worst crisis of VA history to rapidly implode, with shattered psychological safety; breaking the trust with the veterans they serve. It will take a very long time to rebuild that trust with both veterans and employees. Employees who have had to be the best they can be in spite of what is going on.

Even the former VA Secretary, Eric Shinseki, who resigned in 2013, was a retired Army general. He was, in my opinion, shielded by those who exhibited a lack of moral integrity. How could VA leadership across the country allow a situation where secret and false patient waiting lists were created, billions were spent on contract overruns, veterans' claims were shredded, and medical and other facilities operated without proper oversight? Rampant cover-ups are still being uncovered, and retaliation is still the order of the day in VA facilities throughout the country, as evidenced by the inspector general report released in March 2016. One does not have to dig too deeply to see news of hearings in Congress addressing the continuing crisis.

Credibility takes time to attain and maintain. Losing credibility is almost impossible to regain without a lot of soul searching and genuine caring. I do not see total credibility being restored within the VA during my tenure, although many are genuine in their attempts to do so. While I fully admire and respect the current VA secretary, he is in an untenable situation where he will feel the sting of those remaining in power who are just biding their time and riding out the firestorm while protecting their position. VA employees feel the same when managers and supervisors who are charged with violations or retaliation are allowed to return to their jobs without accountability.

The overarching VA Central Office wishes to "engage" employees, but in the meantime, it encourages whistle-blowing through mandated training for managers and supervisors but not for employees. Employees have told me, coast to coast, that whistle-blowing is tenuous and arduous at best, and there is no final accountability of those who actually committed the violations. The VA is keeping the same people in charge of facilities and allowing the managers and supervisors who created this mess to remain, without accountability, and supervise the employees who had the courage to report fraud, waste, and abuse.

I continue to have discussions with thousands of employees across the country, whom I know to be superior performers and who have the right stuff. They have, however, been beaten down by the current conditions, and many experienced retaliatory strikes when either bringing a problem forward or suggesting needed improvements. Diversity of individuals was clearly ignored and extinguished in favor of personal gain. This brings me back to my point. Many employees should have acted with integrity years ago, even at the risk of their positions, but they did not—until just a short time ago. By then, it was clearly too late for the VA to recover quickly, but the others who created this mess still remain employed.

There are unions, yes, but unions typically look out, as they should, for the workers—not for the institution or facility. I believe that, until there is an organizational climate group supported by the director of every facility in the VA system, there will never be a chance for the VA to recover. There should be a much stronger ethic of Guardians of Peers, whereby former service members from each branch would form groups. These groups of peers would actively seek out and support the welfare of their fellow employees, challenging those who act in boorish, illegal, or immoral ways. We need to take back the moral high ground from those who feel they control the destiny of diversity—or just don't care about it at all.

Revitalizing Dr. King's Dream

The Civil Rights movement masterfully led by Dr. Martin Luther King was a perfect example of Guardians of Peers. The movement included all generations from all races and ethnicities, both sexes, and from all parts of the country. People believed and focused upon one idea; the one unifying principle of equality. Everyone involved with the movement desired to view race as inconsequential to the greater cause of equality. Dr. King recognized this through his "dream." There was, however, understanding by Dr. King and others that civil rights were not going to be fully achieved immediately and that it would take ongoing dialogue to fully realize equality. The 1960's atmosphere notwithstanding, and even with congressional acts and executive degrees, peoples' hearts and minds would not be turned quickly. Dr. King himself stated that "If you can't fly, then run; if you can't run, then walk; if you can't walk, then crawl, but whatever you do, you have to keep moving forward." He understood that it was going to take time to do something of this magnitude, even if it was a moral imperative.

Dr. King understood that the "baton" would have to be passed to others in the quest for equality and to shift diversity into its next logical phase in the future. His tireless work in the civil rights arena was demonstrative of a genuine ethic of Guardians of Peers. It was also the guiding light and meaning of diversity and what diversity can do when people act together without division or the need to call attention to race—a world in which, at least to some degree, harmony could exist. Tragically for diversity, the baton was not only halted but also completely lost in time when Dr. King was assassinated. No one from any race has picked up his baton and led diversity and equality to its logical conclusion of inclusion and equality.

Jesse Jackson, who worked with Dr. King, had the potential to become a powerful voice, but instead chose to be lost and remain in a sixties mentality. Some say it is because of the supposed power of voice it gives him to this day. He is, in my opinion, a major disappointment to the civil rights dream, he has failed to galvanize the diversity of people, preferring to promote division and victimhood instead of inclusion. He could have been a healing force but actually began the reversal of the "content of your character" philosophy of Dr. King for personal gain and to keep the money flowing. For example, as reported on multiple news sources throughout the country, during the Ferguson, Missouri, crisis, Mr. Jackson had his workers pass the plate around asking for donations—for his Rainbow Coalition! He received smatterings of boos throughout the congregation and departed Ferguson soon thereafter.

It is simply unbelievable that the old guard of the sixties civil rights movement is still held in such high regard within many circles including black churches and communities. After Dr. King was assassinated, most of the major civil rights leaders created an injustice that continues today. They chose not to enhance and implement Dr. King's dream. Instead, they advanced their own brand of discrimination through messages of inequality, underrepresentation, attacking the "rich," whomever and wherever they may be and creating white guilt whenever possible.

It is a disgrace for all of those who chose to do so; they either knew or should have known better. These so-called leaders and others of like mind at the time of Dr. King had a tremendous, golden opportunity. These leaders actually held the mantle of responsibility to advance our American way of life with dignity and respect for each other; instead, they promoted apprehension, distrust, and brittle emotions, as we have seen even now during the Ferguson, Missouri, and Baltimore, Maryland, protests and riots. Those brittle emotions should not have festered to the level of today if we had all worked together through a genuine discussion on race. Fifty years saw little progress in race relations because invisibility of genuine dialogue of race is still the order of the day in nearly all diversity curriculum.

I remember growing up in the sixties and seeing on television members of all races and backgrounds who held hands as partners demanding civil rights for all. This scenario has been replaced by simmering, dormant emotions ready to explode at any prompting of perceived injustice even if unproven. Adding to this perfect storm are the woeful messages of current "civil rights" leaders who actually seem to enjoy the race-baiting and advancing the victim-hood rhetoric they champion. How can this possibly contribute to equality and diversity and improving race relations?

We repeatedly witnessed on television protesters and looters which started in Ferguson and continued in Baltimore, Milwaukee and other cities with demands of "No Justice, No Peace." That actually translates to "No crime can be committed by (us), and you (them) are guilty, regardless of overwhelming evidence to the contrary." We in the diversity profession lost out because decades of diversity programs and education have not done anything except continue the "us versus them" mentality. These same methods of curriculum continue with such a guilt-laden progressive bent that it would be unrecognizable and deplorable to Dr. King.

CHAPTER 9

Fifteen Key Considerations and Recommendations

Over fifty years has passed since the signing of the Civil Rights Act of 1964. Regrettably, messages of diversity and equality are stuck in a holding pattern of "us versus them" mentality. Despite the efforts to revise the content of diversity curriculum, there is still merely a repackaged "us versus them" aspect to the educational delivery. When I have attended affinity conferences, diversity lectures, cultural celebrations, and the like, the "white-male elephant" is still in the room. The atmosphere predictably affects white males the most, even if nothing is specifically mentioned about this group. I can see it in their eyes when attending other educator's training sessions. It is through the tone of the conversation and multiple messages like "we have a long way to go" or "we are working on more minorities in leadership" that perpetuate the division. Anytime someone says, "we need more of ..." it translates to, "we need less of you (white males)." The number of positions does not change; therefore, increasing representation of one race, ethnicity, or sex exponentially halts or decreases the number of another race, sex, or ethnicity. White males are actually the most negatively affected group when there are special emphasis groups for recruiting monitories and women. The desired outcome is clear; more of us (women and minorities) and less of you; white males.

If you would take a casual look around during your next cultural day event, you will see how few white males are in attendance compared with the cultural group that is being celebrated. Most cultural months are the same. Programmed cultural months throughout the year leave out a white male month. White females are included in women's history celebrations, but there are no months celebrating white males or whites. I am certainly not advocating that we create a "white American" month because I am not a proponent of any of these separate cultural months to begin with. I do feel, however, that we need to consider why we are excluding a significant portion of our population. If we are to have cultural days, they could be periodic cultural days representing several cultural groups at a time who wish to share their culture with others. When you go to a mall, you typically go to look at whatever stores interests you and there are many choices. In my scenario, there would certainly be more of all races and ethnicities in attendance and we could share with each other through dialogue and presentations of cultures represented.

Where do we go from here? How should diversity be presented and defined so that everyone takes away a similar message? Along with my "Gateway to Race Relations World Café Dialogue signature course, I also developed another course, "Cultural Competency—Key Considerations for an Inclusive VA Workforce." I ask audiences to consider what is being presented to them and, as adult learners, take this information back to the workplace with the knowledge that it is a beginning for discovery about each other, our differences, our similarities, and our own unique diversity.

The following are recommendations I have for challenging

current and past diversity curriculum and educational programs. I am also advocating changes to eliminate the EEOC and special emphasis recruitment and outreach programs. Some recommendations may seem like sweeping changes, but I hope you review all of these as key considerations. In addition, those diversity professionals, true diversity professionals, will understand where I am coming from and respect what I propose. There will be pushback and disagreement, of course, but that is what diversity and inclusion is all about: civil discourse and respect.

1. The federal government should eliminate all special-emphasis and recruitment programs.

Why do taxpayers fund these expensive programs that have had little, if any, proven return on investment (ROI) for what they are supposed to do? Rarely, if ever, are training programs associated with these programs evaluated for their effectiveness. Significant funding is provided for appointed special-emphasis program employees nationwide at all agencies. Special emphasis program managers are allowed to use about 20 percent of their work hour time to facilitate their special-emphasis program responsibilities, including cultural days or events. Productivity is certainly affected, and yet the expenditure of time is either rarely monitored or provided for the employee resulting in a lack of accountability for success; whatever that may be.

Tens of thousands of dollars are spent by larger agencies each year to attend conferences, develop minority "partnerships," or conduct technical assistance reviews to identify barriers to employment of minorities and women. It is impossible to track or to validate whether anyone ever filled out an application online to any federal agency through usajobs.gov based upon any of these or any other events that special-emphasis program managers and employees attend. Diversity professionals who attend and participate in these typically state it was a good time or they spoke to a lot of people, etc. What an absolute waste of taxpayers' money. As an example of the objectives of one of these programs, the following is a statement from the web page of the National Institute for Public Health special-emphasis program:

"Special Emphasis Program (SEP) ensures affirmative steps to provide equal opportunity in all areas of employment by identifying barriers to diverse employees (known as special-emphasis groups) from achieving their career goals at rates consistent with the general workforce population. Once identified, the SEP managers (SEPMs) recommend solutions to eliminate these employment barriers and work to deploy strategies to ensure equal opportunity for these diverse employees.

The SEPM is responsible for the development and implementation of targeted outreach and recruitment strategies aimed at improving the representation of minorities, women, and persons with disabilities at the National Institutes of Health (NIH). In addition, our SEPMs recommend a variety of diversity and recruitment strategies to assist with the retention, development, and advancement of these diverse employee populations so that each of them can achieve their full potential."

There is no accountability for the success or failure of any SEPM or the facility if they do not reach expected percentages of women and minorities except to do a *deeper dive* into what barriers must exist. What group is missing from this statement? Again, I do not feel that the answer is to include or create a special-emphasis program for white males. We should, however, eliminate these programs since their effectiveness cannot be measured or quantified. Merely feeling good about your attendance at an affinity conference is not an effective recruitment tool, nor can attendance be quantified as a measurement of successful recruitment. Recruitment is actually accomplished more through word of mouth and current employees' referrals than through attendance at an affinity conference or event.

It actually would be heartwarming to see hundreds of employees who applied to the VA due to the special-emphasis programs created for them. This does not, however happen. I would like to see any evidence that an employee actually applied for a job merely by reading an expensive advertisement placed in minority publications or through attendance at affinity conference. Anyone who is interested in a federal position must apply through www.usajobs.gov. Again, the evidence is not there to support special emphasis programs.

Most corporations and all federal agencies yearly spend countless hours and money on these programs which have limited oversight or accountability except to verify they are in existence and submit reports. By the way, there are biases existing in administering special-emphasis programs themselves. For example, if you have a special-emphasis group for Native Americans/Alaskan Natives, and this group becomes overrepresented by even a small percentage, the "special-emphasis" funding will be cut back. In contrast, the African American special-emphasis program will still exist even if there is substantial overrepresentation of African Americans in the federal government. No convincing explanation is ever provided to me when I ask the question about why we still need these programs. First of all, some diversity professionals are caught off guard, probably never hearing that question asked before. Then the reflex answer typically has been that "we still need these program because these groups were historically underrepresented." At what point will we finally muster the courage to say that we do not require these untouchable programs just because they are historical? And, at what point when full representations occur, does historical become history?

2. Eliminate burdensome requirements for affirmative action plans from corporate and federal contractors and the unbelievably useless federal agencies' Management Directives 715 (MD 715).

Who actually reads these monstrous reports in their entirety? Probably fewer than one hundred people in any agency ever read these, and the size of my agency, the VA, is approximately three hundred and sixty thousand employees. Both laborious reports basically are just "for show" documents, particularly for the federal contractors who dedicate sorely needed resources to maintaining a plan document that is typically seen only by management or the OFCCP. The MD 715 is all report; there is no action associated with it except columns that state what actions were, or anticipated, to be taken, and analysis for identifying supposed barriers. Yet it takes up the valuable time of EEO managers around the country, limiting the time they have to mediate disputes or investigate EEO complaints. Nor is the report read by grassroots employees or front-line managers and supervisors. Without any return on investment, it distracts EEO professionals from much-needed involvement in resolution of EEO complaints at the lowest level. The time of EEO and human resources managers would be better spent on enhancing developing positive benefits, education, and civility, and actually investigating and/or mediating legitimate complaints. This would free those who are responsible for managing an EEOC mandated model EEO program instead of identifying barriers that, you guessed it, will require special-emphasis programs. MD 715 reports are able to depict misguided data through mandated requirements to determine and investigate unfounded barriers and then "drilling down," as the special-emphasis programs say, to find something that has otherwise been found not to exist. It makes my head spin!

What is in it for the white male—or for anyone for that matter? When will this all end? Even former Supreme Court Justice Sandra Day O'Connor stated that affirmative action may not be needed in twenty-five years to promote diversity. A Supreme Court justice that I admire and respect was using diversity interchangeably with racial demographics.

3. Create engaging straight talk, face to face, on diversity, cultural competency, and core values educational offerings including the Gateway to Race Relations World Cafe.

Every organization has core values. The VA, for instance, has ICARE values, which are integrity, commitment, advocacy, respect, and excellence. When I asked two years ago why we were not including ICARE values in a new Senior Executive Service (SES) training program, I was told by senior leadership that SESs already know about ICARE, and it would be a waste of their time to go over these again. Maybe if we had reinforced integrity value, the crisis might have been prevented by leaders who actually did espouse and live by ICARE values. When the crisis imploded throughout VA facilities across the country, Robert McDonald, the newly appointed VA secretary stated on the first day after his confirmation:

"VA has strong institutional values—Integrity, Commitment, Advocacy, Respect, and Excellence—ICARE. If we live by those values, we cannot go wrong. I ask all VA employees to join me in reaffirming our commitment to these core values." He knew, as I did, that ICARE was not being adhered to by many in leadership. So much for knowing or living by these already! If our SES leadership had embraced the core values instead of discounting them, the VA would definitely be in better shape today. Think about it. If the VA SES corps had acted with integrity, commitment, advocacy, respect, while providing excellent care for veterans, no secret waiting lists would have been created, corruption would have been identified much earlier, and retaliation for whistle-blowing would not have been allowed, and the greed of money-driven policies would have not contributed to a moral decline of those in charge.

An Individual's' ability to understand what diversity truly is dependent upon their own level of cultural competency and the development of competencies that apply to everyone, including themselves. The more we understand about differences, the more we can respect how a person might react, think, recommend, etc.

With this understanding, conflicts become a rarity rather than anticipated. Educational offerings should be basic, fun, and alive with learning—not rote memorization of terms or definitions, and they should not be dismissive of certain races.

Face-to-face educational engagement of cultural competency areas is vital to their success. The money saved by eliminating special-emphasis programs could be repurposed for the grassroots employees across the nation, and we could engage tens of thousands more with face-to-face dialogue. There is no better way to gauge the pulse of an organization and instill values, respect, and a sense of pride in the brand than to live it and model diversity, cultural competency, and core values. Employees will notice an immediate difference when managers manage by walking around instead of allowing silos to exist. Don Knauss, the chief executive of Clorox Corporation, stated in an interview with the Washington Post that "If you are going to engage the best and the brightest and retain them, they'd better think that you care more about them than you care about yourself." How absolutely true that is.

4. The word "diversity" should not be so complex; keep it Sesame Street simple.

Mr. Knauss stated in the same interview with the Washington Post that "It's about distilling the complex to the simple; and I've seen leaders fail because they do the reverse, by trying to make things into some intellectual exercise." Diversity definitions and training confound participants so often that if you were to go to ten different diversity classes from ten different companies or agencies, many would have no resemblance to the others. I would shudder to think that we would accept that standard of confusion if the training was meant to instruct Boeing employees, for example, on how to assemble a passenger airline or military jet fighter.

Diversity is a complex, interrelated, and interdependent system in each individual and group. Through educating participants with user-friendly terminology, instructors will not only get the point across but participants will feel included throughout.

5. Keep with the basics, refuse to go to "higher levels," and don't go for the latest fad or *en vogue* word to replace diversity.

It is clearly a mistake to think that once employees have taken a diversity class they are all at the same level of understanding. That does not mean that a company should keep repeating the same class, but it does mean that instructors should not keep creating new levels based upon what they feel that employee should know. Resistance to the training will be in the classrooms particularly with "us versus them" as themes of the curriculum.

There isn't any genuine "getting it" in diversity, but there is getting it right with educational awareness and considerations for the employees. Let's not use stylish acronyms created by the latest diversity consultant or training contractor. Challenge employees' minds with key considerations, and they will accept and understand diversity better than by memorizing terms or creating action plans for themselves. Instructors can screw things up more by making sessions in diversity more complicated or "advanced" (as if someone has already defined basic) or by using terminology that participants will most likely want to forget upon their exit from the class.

6. Do you really want to be referred to with a hyphen as a first identifier?

Why can't we just identify as Americans? If there was ever an element of diversity that just screams "us versus them," it is this one. Sure, there was a time when, say, "Italian Americans" was a theme, but for goodness' sake, let's return to just being American and be proud to be part of this culture. Keep aspects of and pride in your heritage and culture, but now, since you are here, you are an American—or hopefully you are. America is continually developing large, semi-independent cultural groups that are identified with voting, advertising, political power, financial clout, etc.

Political candidates feel they must appeal to the Hispanic, Asian, Indian, or black vote, as if an entire bloc of people of different ethnicities should vote one way or another. Many groups, such as the majority of blacks, vote Democratic for truly inexplicable reasons, since their socio-economic status has worsened under the current president, a Democrat. As individual Americans, we should be able to vote with equal opportunity and not based on the color of our skin or our cultural background. Here again, we see that the overwhelming majority of whites in this country would never use a hyphen with the word American because American is what they feel they are.

7. Eliminate the Equal Employment Opportunity Commission (EEOC).

Many readers will be shocked at this one, and probably their first reaction will be that I want people to experience discrimination or harassment in the workplace. Nothing could be further from the truth. What the EEOC has become though is a bureaucratic nightmare for businesses, the federal government, and actually the courts. Their interpretations of laws create an expectation without ever having to enact new legislation; which should be required.

Many courts have admonished and fined the EEOC, including the Eighth District in EEOC versus Jenner & Block February 9, 2010 which stated that the EEOC's "sue first and ask questions later" systemic approach was not acceptable; the court fined the EEOC $4.5 million dollars for a reckless suit after dismissing the case. The Eighth District, after dismissing another case EEOC Versus CRST February 22, 2012, stated, "How unimpressed the federal courts are with the EEOC's strategy of bringing systemic lawsuits against employers."

The EEOC became a rogue agency years ago and is without

real oversight. They still choose to view complainants as victims and they are idling in sixties and seventies versions of EEO and civil rights while interpreting, incorrectly, versions of the Civil Rights Act of 1964. They are increasingly militant in their approach, refusing to protect the process of equal employment opportunity while expanding through edict instead of law. The process, by law, protects everyone from the complainant to the respondent in a discrimination charge, yet the EEOC advocates primarily, and almost exclusively, for the complainant. The EEOC continually issues edicts with its opinions of certain laws under Title VII of the Civil Rights Act f 1964 and other employment laws they enforce, establishing fear in employers.

Employers who choose to ignore the EEOC edicts and interpretations do so at their own peril, even though the edicts are not supported by law. Employers will take the easy way out and comply, since history indicates that the EEOC will litigate based upon its own interpretation, even if it is flawed. The EEOC's purpose is to be an enforcement agency, not an arbiter of the law. The courts rule against the EEOC routinely, yet the EEOC continues to waste taxpayers' dollars without accountability. I have never seen anything written, spoken, or otherwise from the executive or legislative branches of government that would help curtail this runaway bully. My solution is having the Department of Labor take over the investigation of EEO complaints, enforce the laws, and let the courts establish precedents as they do with other litigation they interpret. The Department of Labor already does this with employment laws for veterans and other labor laws. I believe that the Department of Labor would do a superior job and be fair in its application of EEO law and investigations.

8. Educate, rather than "train" for diversity.

Training is about practice, about skill, about learning how to do things. Education is about fostering the mind by encouraging it to think independently and introducing it to knowledge of the physical and cultural world. While there is some overlap, I believe that educators who develop curriculum are more effective than trainers who program the instruction for definitions, pre- and post-test evaluations, and basically how to do things. How can one "do" diversity? As an educator, I want my participants to take the key considerations I have given them and use their independent thought to further their cultural competencies. I could have them memorize made-up definitions of diversity, inclusion, culture, EEO, unconscious bias, etc., but what does that really accomplish? Instead, I introduce teachable areas or topics as genuine areas of consideration. I attempt to draw upon their understanding and intellect while engaging them further. Encouraging critical conversations instead of silencing dissent is effective in cultural competency and diversity awareness.

A company or agency needs to make carefully considered choices about diversity training. Many times, companies or agencies use outside sources, solicit bids for contracts (selecting, of course, the lower bid), or bring in others who are woefully unprepared for the company's unique employee culture. Using standardized diversity modules that mirror most others except in title or acronym, trainers might be good or really bad, depending on the type of training they have had in this area, if any.

An educator will work with the company or agency and department to gain institutional knowledge. At least, the educator will have a better idea of the organization's pulse, allowing for the creation of an engaging educational program. Diversity and cultural competency education is as vital to an organization as the actual work or product delivered. This is especially true if one has direct customer, student, or patient contact. Understanding, awareness, maintaining respect for others, and having confidence in cross-cultural interactions creates psychological safety and minimizes conflict. What company or agency would not want that return on investment? Or, a company could just choose to save money, use an off-the-shelf train-the-trainer product, and then let that "trained" employee who has not had any diversity experience guide future discussions. I am sure, if you work for a corporation, the board of directors would not support that option. If they do choose this method, they do not understand how diversity should be facilitated and the credibility and competence the educator needs to have.

9. Remove the term "unconscious bias" from diversity education terminology; focus on the cultural competencies that create diversity instead.

Focus on developing cultural competencies that create diversity awareness and basic values. Sure, we all have preconceived associations with things based upon our experiences or preferences; not all of these are discriminatory or personal biases. One may have biases toward certain foods, clothing, or equipment. That does not mean you are personally discriminating against anything. It is hard, for instance, not to have implicit or hidden associations concerning Islam, when most of what we see or hear on the news are descriptions of jihad, terrorists, bombings, etc.

Should people take a step back and become even more aware of Islam, then? Absolutely, I recommend doing so, to gain more awareness and not allow negative news to control all of our perceptions and assumptions. What can you do? Speak to a person who practices Islam; go to a mosque, which I did in Tripoli, Libya; observe an Islamic ceremony, which I also did in Libya, a wedding reception. You gain more appreciation and awareness by encountering someone, rather than discounting and entire group of people immediately and without forethought.

Diversity contractors seize on tragic events, news media, and other sources to push their versions of unconscious bias thought and training. Federal agencies and corporations are teaching a lot of nonsense with this curriculum. They will program the class, however, without students understanding that the target is actually white males. For example, one report, released August 11,

2014, by Professor Dorceta Taylor from the School of National Resources and Environment, University of Michigan, confirmed that unconscious bias exists in the liberal and progressive culture of environmental groups and NGOs, which curb opportunities for minorities by preserving a racially homogenous workplace. This culture makes it difficult for minorities to know about job opportunities. This report was scathing, even though it was directed at liberal, progressive environmental groups. Dr. Taylor further stated that white managers in these organizations struggled with the question of how to make the workplace a comfortable place to work. It is a comfortable place to work when employees contribute their talents, know they count, and know they can count on each other. It is that simple. I question if Professor Taylor is fully enlightened, without any unconscious biases herself. If so, could she let us in on her method of achieving zero unconscious bias? How can she confirm, without a doubt, that someone is unconsciously doing this or that because of their biases?

Angela Park, chief executive of Mission Critical (an environmental NGO) said in support of this report that "this is not rocket science" and that "it is going to take time, obviously but the speed of change and pace of the work (diversity hires) needs to speed up." Being a progressive like Ms. Park does not give a person a pass and doesn't mean that she has eliminated her own unconscious bias. Speed things up? Would she want to make someone a doctor before they finished medical school? I hope that she is referring to hiring the best, rather than just making numbers, but I do not believe this is what she has in mind. This report further supports my contention that the need to teach cultural competencies of diversity rather than guessing whether a person has or does not have an unconscious bias is more relevant. Eliminate unconscious bias and replace the term with implicit association.

10. Drop the need to express excruciating and negative phrases about diversity, which actually have no meaning or purpose. There are many:

"We have come a long way with diversity, but we have a long way to go." I have heard this phrase now for decades; I am getting weary of not only hearing it but of waiting for the speaker to state where the end destination is. At what point are we going to get to this nirvana like destination?

"Even though we are making progress, we know we need to do better." How are you making progress? With what? What do you need to do better? If you want to say that you have done better at recruiting all races except whites, say it; do not mask it with this phrase.

"We need more diversity in our company or agency." Don't let the white-male elephant in the room or just define what you are trying to say. If you really want to say we need more minorities, different races, and fewer whites, then say it. Those who keep saying that we need more of one are also saying that we need less of the other.

"People of color …" This one always hits a note because the message is "all colors except white," of course.

"Browning of America …" Columns such as the previously mentioned "Welcome End to American Whiteness" keep telling everyone to get used to the fact that whites will no longer be the majority, that America is "browning," etc. How would this make members of another race feel if the message were reframed and communicated this way to their race? For example, what if the demographic trend started to reverse, and we were using the phrase "whitening of America"?

"Embrace diversity." This phrase can open up an entire can of worms, especially when people in the workplace merely tolerate each other to begin with. Some people will never be able to get along based on personality alone. Leave out the embrace and replace that word with respect.

"Embracing LGBT" is another phrase that does not take into account the significant percentage of people who have deeply held religious beliefs. It would be next to impossible for someone who has a strongly held religious belief to "embrace" LGBT" or go to a gay pride cultural day, so the quest should be to achieve respect and tolerance from those who would not embrace.

"Our differences, our strength." Not exactly *E Pluribus Unum.* "Out of the many, one" cannot exist just by having differences unless people work together, are understood, included, and respected.

"Celebrate diversity." What are we truly embracing or celebrating? Particularly with celebrate: does that mean people are celebrating the current or changing demographics?

"Diversity is our strength." Diversity comes from within, regardless of color, sex, age, religion, etc.

"Diversity is the right thing to do." Oh, my goodness! This one really gets me going, even after all of these years in the profession. What is right and what is wrong about something that constantly changes and revolves around you every day? What does this overused phrase actually mean to those who say it, anyway? I contend that those who use this phrase do not actually know what the phrase means but are repeating it because they have heard it before.

"Getting it." Some people think they have it or get it (diversity), while others judge those who they feel don't get or just need to get it. What a paradox—and very sanctimonious! No one has the higher moral ground to state someone has something or not. Getting it means completely different things to individuals in the classroom. Sometimes it comes across to white males that they *really* need to "get it" since all other minorities and women get it already.

These phrases, and others like them, contribute to "diversity fatigue." This is mental exhaustion brought on by what I would describe as ineffective delivery of training meant to increase diversity (individuals other than white males) in work settings.

Diversity fatigue can set in even before a diversity class begins; people may be carrying uncomfortable baggage from their prior brushes with cultural diversity workshops.

No matter what upcoming diversity class a person is scheduled for next, that person may already be experiencing a sense of foreboding about the upcoming experience. Participants may have, in past sessions, been made, by the content of the instruction, to feel ashamed, embarrassed, or guilty. Although diversity courses have been revised, that atmosphere is still in the room for white males, only in a veiled format. An ineffective trainer may not be equipped to deal with underlying charged emotions if they were to be expressed. An instructor may let the participants flounder in that instance. Or, maybe the instructor's purpose anyway was to make some participants feel uncomfortable and leave it at that. A diversity professional should not, under any circumstances, make any participant feel uncomfortable. They should always attempt to establish a comfortable and inclusive atmosphere for understanding; that awareness of differences and cultural competency will benefit them now and in the future with cross cultural interactions.

Today, greater emphasis needs to be placed on inclusion, creating opportunities for innovation, and attracting the best talent, but past experiences emphasized affirmative action, "doing the right thing," "getting it"; and understanding "people of color."

11. Create organizational or civic climate groups to discuss issues, concerns, or specific problems that affect the organization or community.

Similar to the Guardians of Peers, these groups typically represent a cross-section of the business or community and create discussions not otherwise held outside of town halls or other formal settings. These groups encompass a larger coalition of voices, share diversity of thoughts, and provide much-needed straight talk. Smaller groups of twenty or less, made up of committed volunteers, will foster enhanced psychological safety, and group members will be able to speak freely on a wide range of diversity topics, including organizational behavior and leadership, civic responses to issues etc. The more discussion and dialogue there is, the more issues with recommended solutions will occur.

12. Engage in dialogue, not debate.

Debate is a notorious word that most people try to avoid. Some people do enjoy debating, but most others do not have the personality or the desire to do so. Debate sometimes gets personal, but dialogue is based on contribution, not confrontation. We should also recognize dialogue's invaluable importance to diversity. It would have been valuable throughout the decades since the civil rights movement to have a dialogue that involved encounters, exchanges, or disagreements among viewpoints, ideas, and different experience and knowledge. Dialogue allows for respect for diversity of perspectives and different views. When only one viewpoint is allowed, dialogue is crushed.

Instead of open dialogue, employees typically encounter more quiet one-on-one conversations in hallways and a lack of willingness by individuals to engage others in conversations about diversity in open forum. An organizational focus on an authoritarian management style creates a debate- and dialogue-free organization. That style enhances individualistic goals rather than productive, cooperative, and consensus-based action. As anyone can see, the authoritarian model is used in diversity education since consensus-building is not part of the individualistic goals. Most people hold very different values systems, which perpetuate the status quo. Diversity educators should realize that critical insights come from those closest to the action; they should not assume that they can push their own personal agendas.

13. Psychological safety should be an institutional expectation.

Dr. Robert Sutton's book *The No Asshole Rule*, which I quote in my workshops (and which should be required reading for some), provides guidelines for creating a civilized workplace and how to recognize assholes. He writes about how organizations allow managers and employees to seemingly get away with bad behaviors, demean others, and generally act like jerks without accountability. The repercussions from experiencing jerks can immobilize individuals and groups. Dr. Sutton also believes that jerks rob workplaces of civility and coworkers of their dignity, at a considerable cost. This behavior also applies to the diversity curriculum and the erosion of American culture and language, as the target of this disdain is white males.

In reviewing Columbia Accident Investigation Board report, August 2003, their extensive investigation revealed the Columbia shuttle disaster could have been prevented by having a psychologically safe environment and eliminating a risk adverse culture. It was apparent that NASA employees were unable or unwilling to communicate the potential hazards due to a flawed safety culture and top down hierarchy unwilling to listen to diverse recommendations for safety. With much dedicated work and inclusion of all employees, NASA turned the previous risk adverse culture around and now has been rated for several years as the best federal agency to work for. We all can do this with dedication to each other and not excluding others!

If one would take a look at diversity discussions and education in America, one would readily see many silenced voices—voices that have been silenced by those who struggled so hard to have their own voices heard. What irony, but also what a mockery of the dream of the greatest civil rights leader of all time: Dr. Martin Luther King!

14. Create and implement a transformational strategy by including white males in the strategy.

Transformational change involving diversity training requires a large amount of contemplation, reflection, input, and prototyping with a lot of room for adjustments. It also requires creative leadership ability and the confidence to manage cross-cultural teams. Successful leaders creatively instill understanding and appreciation of diverse backgrounds, approaches, preferences, and behavior—not all at once but through incremental approaches.

The reality is that few, if any, creative leaders take this complexity seriously. Employees, instead, receive mundane lectures focused on disparate treatment, discrimination, unconscious bias, and white privilege, along with exercises to demonstrate each of these areas. Transformation cannot occur in this type of learning environment. These educational offerings prevent participants from dealing with the challenges of interpersonal differences; they encourage disrespect—not respectful civil discourse.

Transformation is essentially about learning and change; it is often disruptive, risky, and sometimes costly. There are degrees of originality that come with any pursuit of transformation. In the case of diversity, the transformation should have been implemented with incremental improvements. Instead, there continues to be an expectation of immediate and radical transformation of the way we think and interact with each other. That expectation creates an unrealistic learning atmosphere and will not get the job done.

Radical methods of transformation were the preferred method by organizations because these methods were seen as expedient and were less costly. Yet the organizations also need to show in their affirmative action plans that they are making a "good-faith effort" to demonstrate their "commitment" to diversity. The OFCCP and EEOC both audit and review organizational diversity training records to see if everyone has received training. This training, if it has occurred, actually serves as a mitigating factor if a company faces an EEO complaint. Expedience and monetary concerns, however, cannot replace a long-term strategy with effective acceptance of diversity. It takes time and commitment to engage employees and develop awareness of behaviors which mandated diversity training in the first place. Embedding these behaviors into work and life routines requires a different kind of respect for learning. The training atmosphere must ensure an innovative reception of genuine diversity training from all participants who have previously experienced ineffective training.

With courageous leadership from white males, working together with leadership from all races, ethnicities, and religions in this country, we can turn back the hands of time and prevent the looming meltdown of diversity. White males must remove the barriers constructed by others who try to impose "white guilt." There seems to be an enduring premise which created these barriers that the white race exists in a state of perpetual and inexcusable "white privilege." Unless white males are able to break through these barriers, Americans will never be able to complete the dream and we will forever be mired in the past.

Americans, we cannot wait any longer, and we must look forward, not backward. The risks of inaction and the exclusion of white males are unmistakable: look at the results of the last thirty years of diversity programs. I realize that many may equate my message as a dire apocalyptic warning. If you believe that, you are right; it is. We all need to unapologetically agree to not only reverse course but also reprogram our efforts. We will lose any chance of completing the dream if we do not, and the meltdown will occur. The choice is ours as a nation to make, but we must make it now. I have made mine; have you?

How can race relations improve without involving all races in dialogue? Accomplishing extraordinary things in organizations is hard work. People need to feel that they are free to take risks and be rewarded for stepping up.

Employers' diversity departments, particularly in the federal government, became burdened over the last three decades with the addition of special-emphasis and cultural awareness programs. Without forethought or forward thinking, these programs, though some well-intentioned, were created for races and ethnicities and women but excluded white males. Why did this occur, and what did this exclusion accomplish?

Over generations, this exclusion tells the white male that diversity does not apply to him. White males see this perception supported by relevant facts: White males are excluded from cultural-awareness programs; they are the target of diversity classes, whether it is stated or not. Many diversity instructors make the declaration that diversity is a word rarely used today by modern-day so-called leaders of civil rights because everyone, according to them, knows all about diversity! It is not only presumptuous but dangerous to assume that everyone believes in their agendas without question.

Many instructors today prefer to use other buzzwords or speak more of inequality and disparate treatment rather than discussing how people can avoid becoming victims of their own environments. If they did talk about diversity, they would, by all definitions, have to include white males—and that would be an anathema. Who, then, has the problem with race relations as it pertains to diversity? In my opinion, all races do, but civil rights leaders have the responsibility to include everyone. Crises seem to attract those who promote division. The message is lost, but those of us who are champions of the dream will continue to promote the genuine message of equality, as long as there are opportunities to do so.

Women and minorities rarely voice their opinions about racial or gender issues directly to white males, although that is changing. Millennials appear to feel more comfortable with these discussions. When the conversation is muted for white males, however, the result is a lack of racial discussions or expression of feelings and perceptions. White males' voices were silenced long ago by such factors as perceived white guilt, white privilege, threats of discrimination, etc., which forced them out of the conversation entirely. Indoctrination of "us versus them" through historical diversity training has actually altered everyone's ability to participate in these discussions.

In a closed diversity curriculum, a set of ideas and values are defined and imposed as truth in a hierarchical, top-down, institutionally enforced process. Diversity training therefore is monopolized, with dissent and competing ideas labeled as blasphemy and subject to harsh penalties, silencing those who should be part of the conversation. In this environment, diversity exists only as an underground phenomenon and has little to no impact. Unorthodox ideas cannot coexist with a controlled, closed diversity curriculum. New ideas have to be suppressed or the system cannot remain closed.

Diversity in its true sense can never be a reality when the prevailing message is that white males are still, and forever will be, the problem. A race relations conversation requires psychological safety for minorities, women, *and* white males to be effective. I believe that most white males would welcome the discussions; they do so with me in the classroom, in a setting like a World Café, and in other facilitated groups. There is no one bloc of beliefs in white males. White males, however, feel it is not prudent to mention the subjects of race, sex, and ethnicity, for fear of alienating others and somehow being considered politically incorrect. I welcome any discussion in my classrooms and auditorium presentations, but not all professionals have the same mindset or the confidence to do so. The window of opportunity is closing on these sorely needed and crucial conversations, which have been suppressed for decades. Negative perceptions of race relations are increasing in all groups.

The inability of others to understand the faults of their diversity curriculum design is unconscionable. From a targeted curriculum that attacked white males, the blame has been driven underground and relabeled unconscious bias and microaggressions. This training is supported by those who believe that only white males can discriminate and by federal programs advancing the interests of everyone except white males. This unhealthy, negative culture has no possible result but to create a negative spiral downward. Include white males in the discussion and we will see rapid progress in understanding and improvement in race relations. Let's really take a look at the white males' content of their character.

15. Insist on a climate of professional civility

Professional civility does not offer *the* answer to the ills of diversity or race relations, but civility and civil discourse are fundamental behaviors. It is a way to include, not exclude, and to emphasize the importance of all by having everyone feel that their contributions are valuable. The goal of professional civility signals a call beyond our own demands and beyond the scope of any one person. Protection of self-interests in minority and women's agendas has been evident with diversity educators since the inception of diversity education. Denying white males their voices in advancing diversity education became the standard for those incapable of furthering the dream created by Dr. King.

Curriculum designers, who were mostly women and minorities, deemphasized the theme of Dr. King's dream of judging by a person's content of character. They chose instead to emphasize the color of one's skin by focusing upon historical injustices of the past, including slavery, and focused on groups that were underrepresented or underserved and on inequality at all levels. Their incivil exclusion of white males hypocritically disrupts the very professional civility they fought so hard to achieve for themselves. This created a flawed diversity strategy where an inclusive conversation was still profoundly needed. The result was the complete omission of professional civility and any chance for a race relations dialogue. Members of my Baby Boomer generation have had to live with this tragic blunder for decades. Sadly, the younger generations are also experiencing this blunder as well. Professional civility requires moving beyond polar positions and the ability to recognize a middle ground.

Mutual respect is essential to be able to work together and

forge consensus and coalitions on diversity's difficult issues; many of which stir deep and sometimes divisive feelings. Courtesy and decorum foster an atmosphere that allows us to work in good faith to find common ground that appeals to all Americans, not just to those of a particular ideological persuasion. Decorum is essential to allow for deliberation and reasoned judgment and an atmosphere of restraint and thoughtful disagreement. Without this, we have no deliberation, only arguments. I have seen so much of what I love about this country being squandered by those who wish to only advocate for their personal ideological agenda. I prefer straight talk to masked or glossed-over hidden agendas.

Speaking honestly about recommended actions is the embodiment of professional civility. White males have been unable or unwilling to counter the waves of anger, frustration, and revenge emanating from many women and minorities who were empowered to rule the future with regard to diversity curriculum development. One can readily see this today with the "face" of diversity in federal, corporate, and educational institutions. With rare exceptions like me, these positions are filled by an overwhelming majority of minorities and women. The progressive left demanded that the "face" of this new profession *not be* white and male. This barrier, if you would like to refer to it as a barrier for employment, still exists. There are no outcries from civil rights groups to change this overt situation.

Minorities' and women's newly acquired freedoms and rights established equal-protection laws and special-emphasis programs. The goal was to smash historical "barriers" of underrepresentation. All of these advancements, apparently, are unfulfilling to activists, who have an unquenchable thirst for addressing perceived inequality due to prejudice. Truth has been concealed by these activists and replaced with their self-serving agendas that go well beyond the stated purpose of civil rights. The dream was effectively suspended, fracturing any chance of obtaining cultural diversity appreciation and awareness.

Most people in this country who understand the legacy of slavery, know that it deeply affected the lives of black Americans. There are still effects from that legacy. I feel strongly, however, that the legacy exists primarily through misperceptions and choices made versus reality of opportunities. Employment and educational advancements have steadily improved since the 1960s yet other socioeconomic factors created different barriers that prevented achievement. Rampant crime in inner cities, excessive rates of incarceration, dropping out of high school, significant increase in single parents and decrease in marriage rates are not legacies of slavery but the reality of today. There is a significant lack of awareness by all races and, in my opinion, it is due to the lack of race relations dialogue. There is still a tremendous lack of association between whites and blacks, Hispanics, etc., which provides limited opportunities for cultural competency development or appreciation and respect for differences. How can people develop cultural competencies and respect when there was or is little chance to learn about each other and converse?

We could play the infamous "what if" game: What if the internet or cable television had existed, with instant news and documentaries about civil rights. This would have provided much more education for the general public. There has been, in my opinion, substantial change in race relations and awareness, in spite of barriers diversity educators have created. If white males were included in the diversity profession, I believe that awareness and respect would have occurred decades ago, completing Dr. King's dream. Instead, white males suffered with activist-driven curricula that maintained blame, vindictiveness, and exclusion. We will never see change kick into high gear unless cultural awareness training is conducted in an inclusive manner.

Diversity and inclusion, as I state in my workshops, can be a positive dynamic for the workplace. It can also be a tinderbox sitting next to a fire if individuals are not recognized and appreciated for their uniqueness. Conflict theory speaks to unnecessary crisis in the workplace, not all of which are "diversity" related. I have observed, many times throughout my career, trivial differences that override genuine crises or conflict.

Imagine starting your work day with a chorus of "We Are Family" or merely feeling that we are all friends. That is unrealistic at best and can be the start of conflict when even simple misunderstandings occur. Professional civility recognizes that this is just not the case; we are not all friends or family. This is true even when we inexplicably expect people from all diverse backgrounds, some of whom just do not like each other (and never will), to be thrust into a work environment together and "make it happen." We need professional civility in order to avoid conflict and allow employees to be engaged with the work they do. It takes flexibility and people managers (not technical ones) to achieve employee engagement. Just "making it happen" or "just do it" are not strategies but slogans.

16. Create and be a part of the national conversation on race relations.

Americans have been hearing for years that we need to have a national conversation about race, ethnicity, sex, religion, or whatever is causing diversity difficulties in organizations or communities. Historically, many people did have these conversations, but those wondrous flames of discussion and awareness became only embers. After Dr. King's assassination, some conversations continued but only for a very short time. Most Americans felt less than inclined to dialogue, apathy set in, people just did not want to become involved, or they were afraid to do so, especially when political correctness became *en vogue*. These conversations were vital and should have continued. Tragically, they have still not been restored as evidence provided by failed diversity education. After the Ferguson, Missouri, grand jury decision not to indict, people released emotions, including anger, hatred, distrust, sadness, relief, support, and despair. Instantaneously, a collective negative catharsis was unleashed, expressing long-held, deeply embedded perceptions and experiences and increased racial tension throughout the country. I spoke to members of the Ferguson community during the race relations dialogue I mentioned earlier. They stated during the dialogue that racial tension had been occurring for decades in Ferguson. They also stated they learned more in that two-hour session from other races than they had in over twenty years as residents of Ferguson.

We can reverse this trend by supporting a national conversation through a series of World Cafes for Race Relations. We can break down barriers of communication, increase awareness and respect by sitting down with each other face to face and working together through dialogue to address questions that matter. I believe in this method and if you experience a World Cafe, I sincerely believe you will also. I relish being in the arena and ask that you join me to ensure awareness and equal opportunity for everyone.

The sum total of each person's life experiences can swiftly surface in the span of just a few moments. Reawakened racial tensions that had been dormant for decades became visible in many cities over the last two years. Americans of all races, in survey after survey, reported a nosedive of positive feelings about race. The diversity meltdown is now an unmistakable reality.

Mainstream television, radio, and social media contributed to the ensuing rioting in Ferguson, Missouri. Medias repeatedly broadcast, day after day, negative messages, such as the lack of minority representation on the police workforce and city council, profiling, the police force's disparate treatment of minorities, etc. When volatile ingredients are shaken, what results would you expect? A bottle of nitroglycerin comes to mind.

After this and other crisis situations, we hear that we need to have a "national conversation about race." Unfortunately, all we hear is that we need to have one. What exactly is that conversation? There must be a conviction to start one and continue the dialogue. Would everyone want to be involved in this conversation or would we encounter those who are defensive, unresponsive, or unwilling to listen to other viewpoints? Or, as some may imagine, do many minorities and women desire to keep the failed diversity curriculum intact and continue to exclude white males? The World Cafe on Race Relations is a beginning and others can create more events like these to enhance continuing and positive conversation. The positive results outlined in participants' comments spoke volumes for continuing the conversation.

Even if women and minorities considered white males "outsiders" to their interests, they should have had the integrity to promote a safe environment for debate and risk-taking. They did not. I feel that many wanted to include white males but were silenced by those who had the louder voices. The best program would have involved people with a strong set of beliefs in the value of diversity and the importance of unleashing creativity; those who would see white males as part of the solution and not the culprit for all ills affecting other races and ethnicities. Individuals who were being honest in dealing with themselves could expose their own "hidden agendas" and find productive alternative approaches.

Much-needed straight talk conversation requires discussing obvious root causes of minority representation, incarceration, illegal immigration, single parenthood, etc., that are directly impacting racial relations. I want to continue to be part of this conversation with the understanding that the questions that matter will take time to create deeper understanding. The conversation will not be valuable unless all of the cards are on the table and people are willing to contribute their views and to listen without agendas becoming barriers.

As we listen, however, we typically do not hear all of another person's conversation; instead, we tend to formulate our defensive responses while we are listening. This inhibits our understanding of the other person's view. If we thought more like scientists and less like lawyers, we would have much more success: we would listen first, gather the facts that are presented, and form our opinions based upon facts in evidence, rather than react with our own perception of the other person's facts that we did not really listen to.

Everyone involved in these conversations should have the ability to appreciate the value of diverse opinions in developing approaches to achieving goals. All parties need to recognize that they can listen, clarify what was said, and ask questions to gain an understanding of others' opinions—without agreeing. When disagreement or conflict is about to occur, we should deescalate and apply the "agree to disagree" method and depart from the conversation respectfully. We have not and do not have these crucial conversations with current diversity training, where everyone's opinion is respected and debate is encouraged. Decades of diversity curriculum silenced the needed white-male voices and actually hardened other voices.

Much needed critical conversations are ignored and glossed over by curricula that target white males. My advice to white males is to take the time prior to these conversations to understand our own "hot buttons" and triggers and apply reflection and a method to deescalate. Knowing what makes you angry and frustrated will empower you to manage your reactions and respond in a more appropriate manner. Practice self-restraint and focus on your overall objectives in responding to potential conflicts of opinion that will be brought to the table.

I believe the aftermath of recent inner city disastrous crisis situations are obvious indications of thirty years of failed diversity programs. Training ignored real issues and consistently promoted "us versus them" while eliminating straight-talk conversations. Literally hundreds of thousands of diversity awareness, inclusion, and sensitivity sessions have occurred in businesses and agencies. These sessions are still being delivered to employees nationwide and serve to drive racial bitterness, misperceptions, and feelings underground.

Although critical conversations occurred during the 1960s,

the assassination of Dr. Martin Luther King ended or at least suspended them. Employees need to feel psychological safety in the workplace. Psychological safety increases the ability to express opinions. These conversations will never occur or will at best be extremely guarded without it. We need to understand that acquiescence is merely accepting something reluctantly but without protest. No one likes to be forced into this method of acceptance and it bars further discussion because, basically, you waved the white flag of surrender. Leadership and management of corporations and federal agencies are responsible for ensuring that they advocate openness and caring for all of their employees. I believe that there are literally thousands of leaders and managers throughout the federal government who do not fulfill this responsibility.

Civil discourse and debate increase several positive aspects of organizational work life, including critical thinking, intellectual curiosity, engagement, and accountability.

Management and supervisors should welcome differing opinions from their employees with regard to diversity. Reacting otherwise to differing opinions creates a stifled environment and a chilling effect on discussion of issues; while also affecting decisions in many other areas. Interpersonal and manager-employee conflict is minimized when employees feel that they can express ideas and opinions freely without repercussions or reprisal.

Real-time conversations should have progressed to race relations discussions and panels that included white males from all viewpoints so everyone could contribute at the table. This positive scenario never materialized in any diversity program, and curriculum designers put a lid on nearly two generations of emotions that begged for recognition and understanding. Regardless of anyone's views of Donald Trump, his relentless straight talk about issues sparks much-needed conversations. It also elicits reactions, whether agreement or disagreement. We need a lot more of this and the ability to achieve respectful yet critical conversations.

Hannibal ad Portas

The Latin phrase *Hannibal ad Portas* translates as "Hannibal is at the door." The fear of Hannibal became so great in Rome that it was said Roman parents would use this phrase as a way to threaten and scare their misbehaving children. But the threat also contained elements of truth, since Hannibal had won many battles against Roman legions and was actually threatening the gates of Rome before he was defeated. This illustrates the psychological impact Hannibal's presence in Italy had on Roman society, even when he was not at Rome's door. Rome had not previously experienced a military threat of this magnitude.

I have revealed multiple psychological and sociological factors that are creating the equivalent of a meltdown of diversity in America. Americans' common set of cultural values make up our American heritage, yet those same values are melting from within and destroying the very fabric of our nation. It is with great trepidation that I see our cultural values being eroded by a combination of factors described in this book. This creates an urgent crisis situation for the American diversity experiment. Eroding our culture are massive numbers of illegal immigrants, members of some religions who refuse to assimilate to the American culture, and the progressives who support them. Illegal immigrants, who deplete our resources; many refuse to learn the language, they bring illiteracy, and some bring crime, drugs, and gangs to America. I challenge anyone who believes that all illegal immigrants are hard-working people looking for a better life. Most are, but too many are not, as we can see from prison statistics and the exhausting of our resources. The people who are of the second category seek to exploit, terrorize, or live off what other Americans have worked so hard to achieve. Many Americans whose democratic values are being eroded are sitting idly by. Many are low-information voters and vote for those who maintain the status quo or allow a new, declining status quo. Americans and illegal immigrants alike who choose racial and ethnic identities above being Americans grind down the pride of our country. Hyphenating your identity to some other country or ethnicity divides by its usage alone. Religion, especially Christianity, is under a constant attack on the freedom of expression, particularly with rapid social and legal changes, such as LGBT rights and gay marriage. Overt activists who refuse to acknowledge anyone else's religious view of their "group" and assault them with charges of bigotry are, through their comments, bigoted themselves.

Muslims in this country suffer from sometimes unnecessary, unwarranted, and biased slights, yet so many are on the forefront of choosing not to assimilate. Some Muslim communities defend their right to administer Sharia laws over American laws. One of these is zero interest when financing a house, since Sharia law prohibits interest from being charged. Talk about division! Our Constitution has an equal protection clause but it does not allow for an additional set of rules that fall outside of the Constitution's protections.

Self-proclaimed and media-driven "communities of color," whose purpose is to perpetuate separation, object to just about anything that would improve their situation and refuse to take responsibility for their own actions or choices. Since their choice is separation, solidarity, and claims of locked-in inequality; these communities believe the deck is stacked against them. They advocate for either income redistribution or reparations (or both) as remedies. Agitators inside and outside of these communities basically offer only complaints and a victim mentality but no real solutions, displaying anger and opposing collaboration. They feel comfortable with a federal government so large that there would be no dissent but merely benefits to derive. They desire that anyone be allowed to vote without identification, giving them the freedom to vote multiple times.

Most of all, however, white males have been left out of any "national discussion on race," have suffered overwhelmingly in diversity classes with unwarranted charges of overt and covert discrimination. White males are told that they are unconsciously discriminating, even if there is no evidence they are doing so. Somewhere deep inside them lies the heart of a racist within the white male. Decades of diversity classes directed at white males had the intent to bring out uncomfortable feelings and establish white guilt and create internal pain. Diversity education has accomplished this agenda with resounding success. What this flawed curriculum has also accomplished is an entire generation that continues to resist, participates only when told to, or merely joined those who succumbed to "white guilt."

The response of inner-city black populations to police, when their population is causing the disproportionate percentage of crime, is perplexing. In particular, blacks should consider the impact of black against black murder and how that affects their communities. Blacks also suffer from additional social and economic impacts including black males dropping out of high school, significant decrease in marital rates and black females who become part of the 70 percent of black mothers who are single parents. These are proven factors which disrupt the black family structure on its own. If the poverty rate, for example, among blacks is due to whites, why has the poverty rate among black married couples been in single digits every year since 1994?

An open, straight-talk diversity curriculum and events such as the World Cafe method of dialogue can evaluate values from the bottom up on the basis of effectiveness, on what works for each culture or what has not worked. Values serve our American culture. They do evolve, whether religious or secular, and tend to be conserved and passed on through generations, enforced by social custom, and supported by the community. Successful values are influential and can be adopted or adapted to other cultural values

Diverse groups working together have the ability to change and challenge existing social, economic and physical environments. Diverse groups can have a distinct advantage; they have a wider range of ideas, values, and behaviors to draw from when faced with new problems. Counter-survival belief systems, such as those advocated by minorities and women have for decades targeted white males. These values have significantly contributed to the meltdown of diversity in America. Race relations dialogue increases the likelihood that our American values can be saved. It is imperative, however, that all Americans wake up to the dangers our values face with diversity's meltdown.

Diversity needs an infusion of creative leadership from those who have the passion to establish a climate and context open for real and not mandated change. Establishing an open climate, these leaders can then provide a genuine opportunity to open productive dialogue about diversity. With over three decades of diversity related training, the newness of the topic to most is unfathomable. Most people hear the word "diversity," but understand it only from the context of others. Others have manipulated the meaning with their not-so-hidden agendas.

Diversity should be understood, promoted, accepted, and instilled within each of us to the point where we are able to move forward with each other. Instead, we flounder in the past but have newer and even more bitter hidden agendas. I write about these needs in the future tense because we do not have a comprehensive, acceptable, diversity education strategy in place in America—and it shows. We could have addressed problems and achieved opportunities to continue advancing diversity rather than creating chaos but chose to only apply Band-Aids to thousands of wounds.

Rather than relying on only one strategy for diversity education, I unequivocally recommend that an organization have at its disposal a reservoir of alternative strategies, all with a straight-talk, genuine leadership base. Many organizations look to best practices of other organizations. A factor that must be considered, but that is often not evaluated, is that best practices can be ineffective if applied without a deliberative approach and review. Best practices from other organizations may not fit so neatly into organizations with different cultural values and unique employee climates.

Diversity education and management should be accomplished from a cultural perspective. An organization's success in these areas is achievable only when others' values regarding, for example, use of power, dealing with uncertainly, tension between individuals, and masculine-feminine issues are explored with reflective consideration. Leaders who have this deliberative approach of examining culture and climate will see the most effective strategy come into clearer focus. Whatever the ultimate reason for the current state of accelerating racial discord in America; the fact is that it undeniably exists. The issue has to be addressed as a national priority and not ignored or placated with mere sensitivity or diversity training. That, as I have highlighted throughout the book, has not had the desired results.

Most in the diversity profession have deluded themselves. Many feel that over the past thirty years, we have achieved enhanced and substantial racial relations success with the flood of diversity classes using substandard methods. Frayed tensions and news reports daily dispel that belief and there needs to be a complete reconsideration of diversity education's delivery. Progress is a struggle, but relying on curriculum has only enhanced an already difficult struggle and made it worse. We struggled to make a change using pie-in-the-sky mentality instead of realizing that change is always difficult and must be inclusive of all races. Since every participant in diversity should have an active and equal role, disparaging white males constrained the dialogue. Classroom participants developed conscious or subconscious implicit associations with the training and it sticks with them. The bottom line is that all who participate in diversity training must be encouraged to speak their minds and say what is in their hearts. All participants must allow removal of their personal "shields" of sensitivity and perceived or expected political correctness or cultural bias. Doing so allows for free flow of dialogue, civil discourse as well as future action leading to solutions.

The results are undeniable. According to a Pew Research Poll from July 2015, over 94 percent of Americans feel that racism is a big, somewhat, or small problem; only 4 percent feel that it is not a problem. Ferguson and Baltimore are prime examples of racial strife that have been revealed. Similar barriers to race relations existed in Dr. King's time, but they were being addressed; race relations were on a course for positive improvement. Yet that stopped with Dr. King's assassination, when his powerful voice was removed from the discourse. We have to understand that moving something forward is only progress if it continues to go forward. Diversity education has degenerated, due to its inexcusable intent and delivery by eliminating race discussions and inclusion of white males. In order for progress to occur, active members of society have to make a concerted effort. I am, and I hope that others of like mind will join me as well. Curriculum designers should develop criteria through a litmus test of sorts, bringing in viewpoints and experiences from all backgrounds. Greater involvement coming from all perspectives allow the participants to capture the true spirit of development. In short, greater input in the past would have yielded a stronger base of dialogue; unfortunately, this did not occur.

Yes, Hannibal is at America's door, and we should be awakened into taking immediate action. Diversity in America has been great, with its culture, and could be once again. Reality has set in with the boiling point on the other end of the spectrum, and most people remain silent—except for the people who are committed to America's obliteration. Diversity in America is melting down, and there is no denying this fact. Other great nations in history melted down as well, when they allowed their laws, culture, borders, and heritage to crumble without reacting to the causes and crises. Envision a chess match. With America's diversity beginning its meltdown over the last few decades, we are losing this match and are currently at check. Race relations have not improved but are declining; assimilation to the American culture by those from other cultures is decreasing at a rapid rate, yet a national discussion is only now being created. If we acquiesce and ignore these conditions by continuing down our path and making another wrong move on the chessboard, the outcome is already determined. The ending will be a failed American diversity experiment and this game will be over. Checkmate, Meltdown.